PRAGUE

**Philippe Bénet
and
Renata Holzbachová**

JPMGUIDES

Contents

- This Way Prague — 3
- Flashback — 7
- On the Scene — 11
- Entertainment — 36
- Dining Out — 39
- Shopping — 45
- Excursions — 48
- The Hard Facts — 55
- Charles Bridge and its statues — 60–61
- Index — 63

Map

Prague Metro 62

Fold out

Prague

Czech Republic

Hradčany

This Way Prague

Magical Capital

To capture some of Prague's special magic, try to observe this "Golden City" at sunrise, as it casts off its shroud of early morning mist. If you can get to the Charles Bridge before the first throngs of tourists arrive you could almost believe you were back in the Middle Ages. On both sides of the bridge loom dark, rather formidable statues of sandstone, figures from the past looking as if they have gathered here for a secret, otherworldly meeting. The skyline is studded with domes, spires and towers, and in the background, to the northwest, Prague castle stands proudly on a hill overlooking the city.

As the sun begins to shine, and the tour groups lay claim to the city, you will discover that the old clichés are outdated. Yesterday's dignified but fusty old lady has unhooked her corsets and has suddenly found a new lease of life as an elegant and lively socialite—the once grim, grey façades of Prague now glow with a fresh coat of pastel colours.

To restore your energy and get into the mood of the city at the same time, you might be tempted to try a typical breakfast: grilled sausage smothered in mustard, served at one of the street stands in Wenceslas Square. Or you could opt for the more subdued atmosphere of Café Evropa, a temple to Art Nouveau. In the evening, anyone who feels at home in Prague usually adjourns to a crowded, smoke-filled *pivnice* (beer house) for a lager or two. As they say: *Na Zdraví Praho!* To your health, Prague!

The novelist Franz Kafka warned that Prague will not let you go once you have fallen under its spell. It's difficult, indeed, not to be seduced by the charms of this bewitching city, with its dreamy, Italian atmosphere. How to define the melancholy mood that permeates the city? Does it come from the soft golden light shed by the street lamps, from the old cobblestones, the gracefully ornate façades, the winding alleys, the ghosts of history? It's impossible to say.

The best way to discover Prague, and to fully appreciate its colourful patchwork of architectural styles, is on foot. In the Old Town, the central square with its perfect arrangement of houses looks almost unreal, like a stage set. Malá Strana (the Lesser Quarter) at the foot of the castle shows off its baroque

palaces, while Wenceslas Square flaunts its elegant Art Nouveau façades.

When night begins to fall, the "city of a hundred spires" slips back stealthily into the realms of mystery.

Bohemia and Moravia

Prague is the capital of the young Czech Republic, which has just over 10 million inhabitants. The Czechs, of Slavonic origin, are pacific and modest by nature, in the image of one of their favourite literary characters, the Good Soldier Švejk whose ingenuity always manages to triumph over the adversities of life.

While Bohemia, former playground of the Czech aristocracy, boasts a thousand castles and elegant spa towns like Marienbad, Moravia, to the east, is known for its vineyards and its lively folklore. It is carpeted with huge evergreen forests in a pleasant landscape of highlands and lakes, inhabited by enormous carp.

A crossroads of history, Prague was the glorious capital of the Holy Roman Empire during the 14th century. Bohemia and Moravia later formed part of the Habsburg empire, from 1526 to 1918. The country was invaded by Germany during World War II, and following the war remained under communist rule until 1989.

A Society on the Move

After breaking with communism during the "Velvet Revolution", so-named because it was relatively peaceful, the young Czech Republic has eagerly embraced the market economy.

For 40 years, everything was owned by the State. Everyone had enough to live on—just about; everyone had a job, though more often than not the jobs were uninspiring and without responsibility. Franz Kafka's book *The Trial* is a good key to understanding the soul-destroying machinery of the old communist régime.

After 1989, a wave of privatization swept the land. There was a revolution in the economy, and another in the way of thinking. All the values that had been repressed for decades (such as the spirit of enterprise, a yearning for success) became indispensable in the new Czech society.

It is the young people, fresh out of university after the Velvet Revolution, who have benefited most from the change. Today, the leaders of Czech society are mostly in their forties. For their elders, the transition has been

The Municipal House, a splendidly renovated Art Nouveau building.

more painful. The cost of living has risen, and retirement pensions have not kept pace. On top of it all, the old folks now have to pay for their hydrotherapy cures in the spas…

Prague itself was rejuvenated in a relatively short time. In the historical city centre, you will see that the façades have been restored to their original splendour. From 1948, when the state nationalized dwellings as well as businesses, few buildings were adequately maintained. After the fall of the totalitarian régime, many of them were returned to their former owners or their descendants, who, if they had the resources, undertook major renovation. Others were forced to sell to the real-estate speculators.

A Rich Culture

They say every Czech is born with a violin under the pillow. It may well be true. You have only to wander through the alleys of the Malá Strana quarter beneath the castle, where the city dances to the sounds of guitars, flutes and violins, joining forces with chiming clocks and tolling church bells. The Prague Spring festival, the cultural event of the year, takes place from May to June, when the walls ring with music. The wistful atmosphere of Prague has inspired a host of composers and musicians: Liszt, Beethoven, Wagner… Mozart, fleeing Vienna, was afforded a hero's welcome here, and the première of his *Don Giovanni* was held in the Prague's Estates Theatre in 1787. While the composer Dvořák is widely known abroad, it is perhaps Smetana who best represents the Czech ideal, having devoted all his works, including eight operas, to the Czech nation.

Literary creativity flourished with the Prague-born poet Rainer Maria Rilke (1875–1926) and writer Franz Kafka, whose spirit still haunts the city which meant so much to him. Banned during the communist period, he has been reinstated as a national hero: former president Václav Havel once proclaimed during an official visit: "My president is Kafka".

CZECH CHECKING

Some of the best-known Czechs are the composers Antonín Dvořák (1841–1904) and Bedřich Smetana (1824–84), artist Alfons Mucha (1860–1939), writers Franz Kafka (1883–1924) and Milan Kundera (1929–). And also tennis champions Ivan Lendl and Martina Navrátilová; top model Eva Herzigová; film director Miloš Forman; and American Secretary of State under the Clinton administration, Madeleine Albright.

Flashback

Celts and Slavs
Several centuries before the Christian era, the Celts occupied the territories corresponding to the present-day Czech Republic. One of their tribes, the Boii, gave their name to Bohemia.

The Slavs replaced the Celts in the 6th century AD. In the 9th century Mojmír I founded the Empire of Great Moravia, which encompassed Moravia, Bohemia, Slovakia and parts of present-day Austria and Hungary. Seeking to diminish the Frankish influence in his realm, his nephew and successor Rostislav looked to the Byzantine Empire. In 863, two Byzantine missionaries, Cyril and Methodius, arrived to preach in the land of the Slavs. Part of their legacy is the Cyrillic alphabet.

The Czechs, who would eventually dominate the neighbouring Slavonic tribes, settled in Bohemia and, in 895, established their capital in Prague, under their chief Přemysl Spytihněv, founder of the Přemysl dynasty, who built the castle on the heights of the left bank of the Vltava.

Wenceslas
Prince Wenceslas, who later became the patron saint of Bohemia, spread the Christian faith in the 10th century. During his reign the St George Basilica was built in the grounds of Prague Castle.

In 950, the German emperor Otto I defeated the Czechs, and Bohemia was annexed to the Holy Roman Empire. It was not until 1212 that the Přemysl prince Otakar I recovered the throne of Bohemia as a hereditary right. Bohemia became an autonomous state.

Under Wenceslas II, who proclaimed himself King of Poland, the Czech dominions grew in size. The death of Wenceslas III, who survived his father by only a year, spelled the end of the Přemysl line, leaving the question of succession unresolved. Eventually the throne went to John of Luxembourg, son of the Holy Roman Emperor, through his marriage to Elizabeth, the daughter of Wenceslas II.

Imperial Capital
In the middle of the 14th century, under the rule of John's son Charles IV, Prague became the administrative and cultural centre of the Holy Roman Empire. Charles, who married Blanche of Valois and carried Přemysl blood through his mother's lineage, was grandson of the German emperor and

Near Prague Castle, the Strahov Monastery houses the Museum of Literature, a veritable monument to books.

cousin of the King of France. He was an erudite ruler and a patron of the arts. He had the castle rebuilt and enticed the best architects of Europe to Prague, to embellish the city in Gothic style. The Frenchman Matthias of Arras designed St Vitus's Cathedral, while Charles Bridge and the tower at the Old Town end are the work of Peter Parler. Charles University was founded in 1348, and Prague soon become the most important city in Central Europe.

Jan Hus

The successors of Charles IV, in particular his son Wenceslas IV, were not quite up to the task of ruling the Czech kingdom. In the 14th century a Catholic priest, Jan Hus, a forerunner of Luther and Calvin, denounced the opulence of the Church and the shameless trade in Indulgences. In 1402, he became the preacher at the Bethlehem Chapel in Prague, then in 1409, rector of the Charles University. His ideas earned him excommunication from the Church in 1412. Having faith and trust in Wenceslas IV, who promised him protection, he went to the Council of Constance two years later to defend his ideas. Refusing to renounce them, he was taken prisoner and burned at the stake in Constance in 1415.

This execution sparked a revolution which was to mark the country's history profoundly. Today, Jan Hus remains a national hero: the anniversary of his death has become a holiday and the Czech clergy has been campaigning (unsuccessfully, so far) for his canonization.

The Habsburgs

In the musical chairs of royal marriages and successions, the crown of Bohemia fell to the Habsburgs in 1526. Vienna was preferred to Prague as their capital, Catholicism was imposed on the Czech people and the Renaissance style on their architecture. Under Rudolf II (1576–1611), who surrounded himself with a glittering court, Prague once again became the capital of the Empire.

The Protestant Czech nobility had significant differences with the House of Austria, and matters came to a head when, on May 23, 1618, representatives of the Protestant estates hurled two imperial governors out the window of the Castle chancellery. The "Defenestration of Prague" (in fact this was not the first time this expedient method was used to settle disputes) sparked the Thirty Years' War. The estates of Bohemia were ultimately defeated in the Battle of the White Mountain. Numerous executions followed in the Old Town Square, and Bohemia lost its autonomy. Part of the Czech nobility was exiled.

An underground movement to revive the Czech national identity was set up around 1780, as intellectuals became dedicated to the defence of the Czech language and literature. In 1868, the construction of the National Theatre, built thanks to donations from all over the country, symbolized the Czech people's new-found pride. Czech architecture and music enjoyed a revival.

Thanks to strong economic development at the beginning of the 20th century, Bohemia became the industrial hub of Austria-Hungary, and factories such as Škoda hummed with activity.

Independence

After World War I, the first Republic of Czechoslovakia was proclaimed on October 28, 1918 by Tomáš G. Masaryk. The territories of Bohemia, Moravia, and Slovakia were thus united, and the Czech people could at last enjoy an uncensored press, freedom of expression and other benefits of democracy. The economy continued to prosper and culture flourished during the 1920s, when Czechoslovakia was as highly developed as

Great Britain. There remained the problem of disenchanted German, Hungarian, Polish and Ukrainian minorities. The good times didn't last long, for war was brewing over the border.

Hitler laid claim to the Sudetenland, in Bohemia, which had a strong German community. Let down by France and Great Britain at the Conference of Munich in 1938 (in spite of past treaties of intervention in case of conflict), the Czech president Beneš had no other resort but to cede the disputed territory. The German army invaded the country.

Prague was liberated by the Soviets on May 9, 1945, and more than $3^1/_2$ million Germans were expelled. The Czechs, remembering the 1938 betrayal by the French and British, turned to the Soviets; in the 1946 elections the Communist Party obtained 40% of the vote. Industry and commerce were nationalized and freedom of expression was abolished. Many fled the country. Those who stayed at home witnessed the purges and trials of the Stalin era in the 1950s. The country acquired a new, unequivocal name in 1960: the Socialist Republic of Czechoslovakia.

In 1968, the winds of freedom blowing across Europe were felt in the east. Supported by a population eager for change, the new secretary general of the Communist Party, Alexander Dubček, advocated a "Socialism with a human face". It was the flowering of the Prague Spring. In response, on August 21, 1968, Soviet troops invaded the country to ensure its "normalization". Dissidence continued throughout the 1970s, leading to the birth of the Charter 77 group, formed by intellectuals opposed to the regime.

The Velvet Revolution
In 1989, the fall of the Berlin Wall unleashed a tidal wave of hope throughout Eastern Europe. A student demonstration inspired by the Civic Forum, a dissident movement, gathered 30,000 people in Prague to acclaim Václav Havel, an intellectual who had spent several years behind bars. Havel was elected president of the Republic on December 30, 1989, the culmination of the Velvet Revolution. On January 1, 1993, Czechoslovakia split into Slovakia and the Czech Republic.

Under prime minister Václav Klaus the Czech Republic swung towards liberalism, but the people voted against him in 1997. President Havel retired at the beginning of 2003. The Czech Republic became a member of the EU in May 2004 and presides over the community for the first term of 2009.

On the Scene

The best way to explore the historical centre is on foot, observing the city's amazing mixture of architectural styles—Romanesque, Gothic, Renaissance, classical, baroque, Art Nouveau, cubist. When looking for an address, bear in mind that the words for "street" or "avenue" are never indicated on signs. Thus Národní 14 means 14, Národní Street. On the other hand, the word for square, *náměstí* (abbr. *nám.*) is frequently used. Václavske náměstí 14 is 14, Wenceslas Square.

WALKS

Prague is made up of four towns which were united administratively in 1784: on the left bank of the river, dominating the town, is Hradčany, the castle district and, at its feet along the river front, Malá Strana, the Lesser Quarter. On the opposite bank are Staré Město, the Old Town, and Nové Město, the New Town. Our walking tour starts in the New Town, on Wenceslas Square. Follow Na Příkopě Street, then Celetná to reach the Old Town Square. A maze of crooked streets and alleyways surrounds this square, without doubt the most attractive in Prague. Next, heading along Karlová, you arrive at the famous Charles Bridge.

On the other side of the river, you should take time to explore Malá Strana, a peaceful quarter of baroque palaces, stately embassies and elegant gardens. Finally, climb the hill to the imposing castle and its surroundings, from where there are remarkable views over the city.

NOVÉ MĚSTO

Planned from the 14th century, the New Town was fully renovated in the 19th and 20th centuries.

Wenceslas Square F 4–G 5
- Václavské náměstí
- Metro Můstek or Muzeum

Founded in the 14th century and largely remodelled in the 20th, this is the commercial and banking centre of the Czech capital. It is not really a square but a wide avenue stretching from the National Museum to the edge of the Old Town. At the museum end looms the bronze equestrian figure of Prince Wenceslas, surrounded by the statues of four Bohemian saints. The square has witnessed several significant historical events: the 1918 demonstrations that led to the establishment of an independent state; the self-sacrifice of the young Czech student Jan Palach, who burned himself to death in 1969 in protest against the Soviet presence; the moving speech by Václav Havel in 1989 that ushered in a new era. There is a small, and moving, memorial to Jan Palach just in front of the Wenceslas statue. The National Museum, dominating the scene with its golden dome, stands on the other side of a busy main road built contrary to all common sense during the communist regime. At the far end of the square, at No. 1, is the Koruna Palace. At No. 34, the Wiehl house boasts a neo-Renaissance façade. To the right, Na Příkopě borders the Old Town. On the left, you reach National Street and the National Theatre.

National Museum G 5
- Národní muzeum
- Metro Muzeum
- Daily Oct–April 9 a.m.–5 p.m, May–Sept 10 a.m.–6 p.m.
- Closed first Tuesday of the month

Flaunting a somewhat intimidating neo-Renaissance façade, this imposing building houses a monumental stairway which leads to the Pantheon. Here the country's history is illustrated by a series of busts and statues of famous men. There are also interesting collections of minerals, prehistoric objects, zoology and palaeontology.

On the Scene

Hotel Evropa G 4
- Václavské náměstí 25
- Café 9.30 a.m.–11 p.m.
- Tel. 224 215 387
- Fax 224 224 544

The Hotel Evropa is a monument to Art Nouveau, a style inspired by baroque which flourished between 1897 and 1910. Its famous façade is awash with gilded lettering and floral motifs, mosaics, and wrought-iron balconies. If the hotel has a somewhat faded charm, the café on the ground floor will take you back to the carefree atmosphere of the early 20th century. Peep into the restaurant to view Art Nouveau style in all its splendour: wrought-iron banisters, mahogany woodwork, stained glass, gilded bronze caryatids and a green glass ceiling.

Church of Our Lady of the Snows F 4
- Chrám Panny Marie Sněžné
- Jungmannovo náměstí

Heading down from Wenceslas Square, turn left on 28. října Street, to reach Jungmannovo Square. Erected in 1347, this church was "baroquified" in the 18th century. The main altar is the largest in Prague. The gardens, bordering a former Franciscan convent, are a haven of peace within the New Town.

National Avenue E–F 4
- Národní

Turn left at the end of Wenceslas Square into National Avenue, leading to the river. Note some of the fine façades, in particular the gilded Art Nouveau architecture of the former Prague Savings Bank at No. 7 and the Topič house, No. 9.

National Theatre E 4
- Národní divadlo
- Ostrovní 1

Built between 1868 and 1881, this neo-Renaissance building dominates the Masaryk riverside quays. It is striking both inside and out, and was rebuilt thanks to private donations following a fire at the end of the 19th century. The National Theatre symbolizes Czech national identity and pride.

Na Příkopě F–G 3

If you turn right at the northern end of Wenceslas Square, you enter Na Příkopě, a street full of banks. At No. 10, note the Sylva-Taroucca Palace which today houses the casino; at No. 14, the 19th-century Church of the Holy Cross; at No. 20, the Živnostenská Banka, whose premises are a splendid neo-Renaissance palace. At No. 22 stands the Slavonic House, originally baroque and later remodelled in the classical style.

On the Scene

Mucha Museum G 3
- Kaunický palác
- Panská 7
- Daily 10 a.m.–6 p.m.

This museum displays more than 80 works by the painter and decorator Alfons Mucha: paintings, photographs, charcoal sketches, pastels and lithographs, in addition to personal items. There's an attractive shop.

Born in Moravia in 1860, Mucha started out as a stage-set decorator. He went to study in Munich, then moved on to Paris, where he eventually acquired fame and fortune. At first he made his living as illustrator for the newspaper, *La Vie parisienne*. In 1894 the French actress Sarah Bernhardt chose one of his innovative designs for a poster, and from then onwards, he never looked back. Mucha is famous for his sensual paintings of willowy women with long, loose locks of hair. After a disappointing trip to New York, Mucha returned to Prague in 1910, where he completed a well-known series of twenty paintings portraying Czech mythological and historical themes. He also decorated the Municipal House and designed the stained-glass windows in St Vitus's Cathedral. Mucha's grandson gathered together his works and created the Alfons Mucha Foundation in 1992.

Municipal House G 2
- Obecní dům
- Náměstí Republiky 5
- Tel. 222 002 101

At the end of Na Příkopě, you reach Republic Square, site of this splendid building in the purest Art Nouveau style. It has been restored to its former splendour and is well worth close inspection. Notice the floral motifs, the ornate stucco, the ironwork wrought into delicate tendrils, leaves and flowers. The colourful semicircular pediment is adorned with an exquisite mosaic, *A homage to Prague*.

The Municipal House was built as a cultural centre at the beginning of the 20th century, on the site of the former royal palace, which had burned down. Fashionable sculptors including Václav Myslbek, and painters such as Alfons Mucha and Max Švabinský took part in its design. Although the Mucha Hall is not normally open to the public, the Smetana Hall with its ceiling painted by František Ženíšek is used for concerts. The building now houses two restaurants, the Francouzská (French) Restaurace and Plzeňská Restaurace in the basement, where display cabinets are filled with beautiful Art Nouveau jewellery and glassware. The Kavárna Café was known as a meeting place for intellectuals.

Among the treasures in the Mucha Museum is this 1911 poster of Princezna Hyacinta (detail).

It's a good address for a casual drink.

Powder Gate G 2
- Prašná brána
- Apr–Nov daily 10 a.m.–6 p.m.
- Admission fee.

Next to the Municipal House stands a forbidding gateway of dark and gloomy stone. A narrow stairway leads to the top of the tower from where you have a view over the entire Old Town. The tower served as a gunpowder store in the 18th century.

Walk through the archway to reach the Old Town, by Celetná Street. This marks the beginning of the Royal Way, the route followed by the kings during their coronation ceremony.

STARÉ MĚSTO

The Old Town developed in a bend of the river during the 10th century. It has retained its medieval air and timeless charm.

Celetná Street F–G 2

Lined by Gothic houses with added baroque details, Celetná is one of the oldest streets in Prague. The façades of Nos. 36, 23 and 21 are particularly handsome.

At No. 34, the House of the Black Madonna is considered a model of cubist architecture (exhibition on Cubism upstairs). The pediment of the building at No. 22 is adorned with a sign in gilded letters in French which means: "Jewellers by appointment of His Majesty".
At No. 12, under the porch of the baroque Hrzán Palace, wander into Hrzánská passageway. Don't miss the magnificent Sixt House at No. 2, with its busts of emperors.

Old Town Square F 2
Staroměstské náměstí
Celetná Street takes you to the most beautiful–and the busiest—square in Prague, which in the Middle Ages was a marketplace and where duels were fought, and where today most of the street performers gather.
It looks slightly unreal, like a theatre set, with its colourful cut-out façades and red tile roofs. All kinds of styles are represented: Gothic porches, Renaissance frescoes, baroque pediments…
The Old Town Square is overlooked by the belfry of the Town Hall to the west, and the turreted towers of Our Lady of Týn church to the east. In the centre of the square stands the memorial to Jan Hus, the Catholic priest who spoke out against the extravagance of the Church in the 14th century, and who became a national hero after being burned at the stake.
Have your camera ready to capture the exquisite façades: that of the Štorch House at No. 16 (late-19th century) can be recognized from the fresco depicting St Wenceslas as a triumphant knight.
At No. 17, see the House of the Stone Ram, whose portal dates from the 16th century, and the 14th-century House of the Stone Table.
To the left of the Týn church, at No. 12, stands the Goltz-Kinský palace, perhaps the finest example of rococo style. Count Goltz commissioned it from the Italian architect Anselmo Lurago in the 18th century. Next door to the Goltz palace, the House of the Stone Bell dates from the 14th century. Don't miss the lovely façade of the building at No. 6.

Our Lady of Týn F 2
Kostel Matky Boží před Týnem
Staroměstské náměstí 14
Pass under the arches of the Týn School (built from the 14th–16th centuries) and the 18th-century House of the White Unicorn to reach Our Lady of Týn, built on the site of a former 10th-century church belonging to a hospice reserved for traders. Týn was a Hussite church, but since the Counter-Reformation

it became a Catholic bastion, and a baroque décor soon crept in. Of particular interest are the paintings by Karel Škréta, the high altar, and the altars of St Barbara and St Joseph.

Courtyard of the Traders of Týn F 2
The Tynská alley which runs alongside Our Lady of Týn wanders through a maze of alleyways and courtyards. The façades of the apartment buildings were recently, and attractively, restored. The merchants traded in the the Týn courtyard up to the 18th century.

Estates Theatre F 3
- Stavovské divadlo
- Ovocný trh 1

Železná Street starts at the Old Town Square, passing alongside the imposing Carolinum building (the administrative centre for the Charles University), to end at the Estates Theatre, also known by its former name, Týl Theatre. It was built between 1781 and 1783 in the classical style. The first performance of Mozart's *Don Giovanni* was staged here in 1787.

Old Town Hall F 2–3
- Staroměstská Radnice
- Staroměstské náměstí 1
- Tel. 724 508 584
- Mon 11 a.m.–6 p.m.
- Tues–Sun 9 a.m.–6 p.m.
- Guided tours available

The Old Town Hall was founded in 1338 and developed throughout the centuries to match the city's growth in size and importance. Its most obvious highlight is the astronomical clock. The Old Town Hall is made up of several buildings, including the House of the Minute, with 17th-century sgraffito decorations. The Kříž House has a beautiful Renaissance window and a baroque grid with the inscription: Praga Caput Regni (Prague, capital of the realm). Also note the series of 15th-century coats of arms on the façade.
The guided tour takes in the lobby, the 14th-century Council Chamber and the Session Hall. It's well worth paying the small fee to visit the top of the tower: the view over the rooftops of the Old Town and of the castle hill is superb.

Astronomical Clock F 2
- Staroměstské náměstí

Dating from 1410 and modified in the 16th century, the astronomical clock consisting of two circular faces is the most curious sight in the square. The upper dial represents the Earth, in the centre, with the planets orbiting around it. The face below, showing the months and the signs of the zodiac, dates from the 19th century. Above the two is a mechanism activating various characters and symbolic objects which burst into activity every hour between 9 a.m. and 9 p.m. Christ and the Apostles appear, then vanish. A gong sounds, and Death brandishes its scythe, tolls the knell and turns over the hour glass. Then it's the turn of Greed to show his purse, and Vanity admires himself in a mirror. A Turkish prince shakes his head to indicate that he doesn't yet want to abandon combat, an allusion to the Turkish invasion of Central Europe in the 16th and 17th centuries. Then a cock spreads its wings and crows in a raucous finale.

St Nicholas Cathedral F 2
- Chrám svatého Mikuláše
- Staroměstské náměstí
- Daily 10 a.m.–4 p.m.

The cathedral is located on the corner of Paris Street (Pařížská). The interior is especially fine, with its galleries and arcades, not to mention the sublime fresco in the dome. German merchants built a Gothic church on the site in the 13th century. Today, St Nicholas is a Hussite church.

Pařížská F 2
Leading off Old Town Square, Paris Street is lined with lavish turn-of-the-century buildings which replaced the small houses in the Jewish quarter, at one time enclosed within a ghetto.

JOSEFOV
Arriving in Prague in the 10th century, the Jewish traders were gathered into a single quarter. Their rights were recognized by the Emperor of Austria Joseph II (1780–90), and thus the Jewish Quarter became known as Josefov, in his honour. But the Jews did not obtain equal rights until 1867. Apart from a few well-to-do money lenders, most were poor and lived a cramped existence in the ghetto. The maze of winding alleys and tiny houses was finally razed in 1892.

Jewish Museum E–F 2
- Židovské Muzeum
- Maisel, Pinkas, Klaus and Spanish synagogues. Guided tours (2 hr) from the Maisel synagogue.
- Daily except Sat and Jewish holidays,
- Nov–March 9 a.m.–4.30 p.m.,
- Apr–Oct 9 a.m.–6 p.m.

The Jewish museum was created in 1906. In 1942, the Nazis decided to assemble the works of art and religious objects left by members of 153 local Jewish communities, many of whom had been deported. The museum became the property

of the state under the communists and it wasn't until 1994 that the Jews recovered their possessions. This museum, which today has one of the world's largest collections of Jewish art with more than 40,000 objects and 100,000 books, is housed in three synagogues.
The entry ticket also gives access to the old cemetery and the Old-New Synagogue.

Maisel Synagogue E 2
- Maiselova synagoga
- Maiselova 10

Reconstructed in neo-Gothic style on the site of a 16th-century synagogue, the Maisel contains an impressive collection of gold, silver and pewter objects used in Jewish ceremonies.

Pinkas Synagogue E 2
- Pinkasova synagoga
- Široká 3

This synagogue is at the bottom of the old Jewish cemetery. The foundations date from the 11th century and were modified in 1625. The walls were chosen as a memorial in honour of the victims of the Holocaust, whose names are inscribed here.
Do not miss the heart-wrenching exhibition of drawings made by children in the Terezín deportation camp, supposedly a model camp.

Old Jewish Cemetery E 2
- Starý židovský Hřbitov
- Entrance through the Pinkas Synagogue, Široká 3

The forest of Gothic, Renaissance and classical gravestones planted in the ground seem to be struggling for space. The oldest tomb here is that of the poet Abigdor Karo, who died on April 25, 1439. From the 15th century up to 1787, graves were laid one on top of the other in this cemetery, sometimes reaching twelve superimposed layers. It has been estimated that this is the final resting place for some 200,000 people. On certain stones, carved images refer to the trade of the occupant; a mortar, for example, indicates a pharmacist.

Klaus Synagogue E 2
- Klausová synagoga
- U starého hřbitova 1

Exposition of objects related to Jewish customs and traditions.

Old-New Synagogue E 2
- Staronová synagoga
- Červená 2

The oldest vestige in the Jewish quarter is also the oldest synagogue in Europe, simply called the "new synagogue" when it was built in the 13th century. Its small size gives a good idea of the tiny dimensions of the other houses in the ghetto. It is still used as a place of worship. The hall is covered with a 6-ribbed vault supported by two octagonal pillars. Notice the porch (the oldest element of the building), the 16th- and 18th-century wrought-iron chandeliers, and the grid around the cantor's platform which dates from the 15th century.

Jewish Town Hall E 2
- Židovská radnice
- Maiselova 18

Next to the Old-New Synagogue, at the top of a house built in the 16th century and refurbished in the 18th, is a clock with Hebrew figures whose hands turn anti-clockwise (Hebrew is read from right to left).

Spanish Synagogue F 2
- Španělská synagoga
- Vězeňská 1

This synagogue was built in 1868 in a remarkable Moorish style. The central area is surmounted by an elegant dome, while the walls are intricately decorated with stucco arabesques and oriental patterns. Objects used for worship and documents tracing the history of the Jewish community on the lands of Bohemia and Moravia are displayed in glass cases. On the first floor is a poignant exhibition of photographs illustrating the old Jewish town.

St Agnes's Convent F 1
- Klášter Sv. Anežky České
- U milosrdných 17
- Tel. 224 810 628
- Daily except Mon
- 10 a.m.–6 p.m.

The convent is the seat of the Museum of Bohemian and Central European Medieval Art. The setting alone is bewitching: a Gothic building dating from the 13th century. The exhibition traces the history of medieval art from the 13th to 16th centuries. Among the 270 works on display, do not miss

---

GOLEM

Every Czech, young and old alike, is familiar with the legend of the Golem, an imaginary character whose mission was to defend the Jewish community. The legend goes that Christians were becoming hostile towards the Jews, believing they made human sacrifices during their religious festivals. To protect the Jews from reprisals, Rabbi Löw fashioned out of clay a being with superhuman powers, the Golem, which obeyed him. But one day the rabbi forgot to give the Golem its instructions, and the vengeful creature went on a destructive rampage. Löw was obliged to remove the Golem's magical powers, and it turned back to clay.

the collection of carved Madonnas, and the three series of wood panels by the Master of Vyšebrod (around 1350), Master Theodoricus (end of the 14th century) and the Master of the Třeboň altar (1380–85).

TO CHARLES BRIDGE

For nearly four centuries the Charles Bridge, built in the 14th century, was the only way to cross the Vtlava river.

Lesser Square F 2–3

From the Old Town Square, pass in front of the Astronomical Clock and the Old Town Hall to reach Malé náměstí, lined with attractive Renaissance and Gothic façades. The well in the centre of this square, closed by an elegant wrought-iron grid, dates from 1560. At No. 11, turn into the gallery that leads into a network of winding streets, with many of the buildings boasting freshly renovated façades in a variety of pastel colours. The pharmacy U Zlaté Koruny, at No. 13, was built in 1887; the interior is superbly decorated in dark wood (it's now a jewellers). At No. 3, the Rott House, adorned with neo-Renaissance frescoes by Mikoláš Aleš, houses a luxury food store. In the wine cellar you can admire Romanesque remains and bottles of first-class vintages from all over the world.

Karlova and Husova E 3

Narrow Karlova Street threads its way to Charles Bridge and is lined with interesting shops and buildings. At No. 8, note the stone porch of the Unitaria Palace. An inscription on No. 4 states that Johannes Kepler, the famous alchemist to Rudolf II, once lived here. Turn into quieter Husova Street: the imposing porch at No. 20 is flanked by a pair of gigantic Atlas statues. This is the Clam-Gallas Palace, housing the city archives. Note the attractive fresco on No. 15, representing a couple of wine-makers holding a bunch of grapes. And don't miss U Zlatého Tygra at No. 17, a typical noisy, smoky watering hole.

Bethlehem Chapel E 3

- Betlémská Kaple
- Betlémské náměstí
- Daily (except Sun)
- Apr–Oct 10 a.m.–6.30 p.m., Nov–March 10 a.m.–5.30 p.m.

A short detour along Husova, to the left, takes you to the Bethlehem Chapel, rebuilt in 1950 according to ancient manuscripts and the original plans. Jan Hus preached here in 1402.

St Giles's Church E 3

- Kostel Svatého Jiljí
- Husova 8

Built in the 14th century, this Gothic church was a Hussite parish before it passed on to the Dominicans in the 17th century. The interior was "baroquified" in the 18th century. Observe the pilasters and pillars, and the ceiling frescoes. At one time the church was patronized by French merchants, and some of the altars have inscriptions in French.

Klementinum E 3
Karlova 1
Baroque library and astronomical tower open to the public daily
Jan–Apr, Oct–Dec 10 a.m.–6 p.m
May–Aug 10 a.m.–8 p.m
Sept 10 a.m.–7 p.m.

In the 16th century, the Jesuits undertook construction of a college, two churches and two chapels. Today, researchers and students work in the libraries whose shelves plow beneath the weight of 6 million volumes. Concerts are organized almost every day in the Mirror Chapel. The baroque library, completed in 1772, holds some 20,000 philosophical and theological works, the oldest dating back to 1600. The 18th-century trompe-l'œil ceilings are remarkable, as are the fascinating 17th and 18th-century globes. Narrow staircases lead up to the top of the tower overlooking the Old Town. Built around 1750 and equipped with two 18th-century telescopes, it has been used by generations of astronomers and mathematicians.

Knights of the Cross Square E 3
Křižovnické náměstí

Continuing along Karlova you reach this square near the river and Charles Bridge. On your right, a statue of Charles IV stands outside the Church of St Francis (Kostel Sv. Františka), which features sublime ceilings and a superb baroque organ, dating from 1702. The concerts held in the church are outstanding.

CHARLES BRIDGE AND THE RIVER BANKS

As you cross the Charles Bridge, built in the 14th and 15th centuries, a wonderfully romantic view unfolds on either side of the river. On the left bank, the castle towers over the city. Below it the baroque palaces of Malá Strana, the Lesser Quarter, huddled at one end of the bridge, are capped by red-tiled roofs: a genuinely medieval setting, unique in Europe.

The bridge is one of the liveliest places in Prague, thronged with visitors, hawkers and street performers all day long and well into the night. To have it all to yourself, get up early and see it at dawn.

On the Scene

Charles Bridge D 3

- Karlův most
- Tower (Old Town side) daily
- Jan–Apr, Oct–Dec 10 a.m.–7 p.m.
- May–Sept 10 a.m.–10 p.m.

The bridge is undergoing restoration work, spanning several years, but remains open to visitors. Two dark, crenellated towers rise on either side of the bridge. On the right bank, the Old Town side of the river, the first of the towers (Staroměstská Mostecká Věž), was designed by Peter Parler in the 15th century. A narrow stone stairway leads to the top, offering an interesting view of the bridge and castle. On one side of the tower you can see the sculpted heads of Wenceslas IV, St Vitus and the Emperor Charles IV. Constructed of dark sandstone blocks, the bridge measures 520 m (1,700 ft) in length and is 9.5 m (31 ft) wide. Its entire length is adorned with thirty statues added in the 18th and 19th centuries, though most of those you see today are copies of the originals (see pp. 60–61).

The bridge used to link two independent townships, Malá Strana and Staré Mesto. Charles IV commissioned the architect Peter Parler to replace the old Judith Bridge, which stood on the same site and had been swept away by floods. Work started in 1357. Recent analysis has revealed that eggs, milk and wine were added to the mortar as a binding agent.

A strange punishment was enacted in front of the third statue to the left, representing a Pietà: it's said that bakers caught skimping on the flour would be locked in a cage and lowered into the freezing waters of the Vltava.

In the middle of the bridge is the only bronze statue, and also the oldest, which portrays St John Nepomuk. The saint is shown holding a crucifix, and around his head is a halo and stars. A plaque indicates the place where Jan Nepomucký, the cathedral vicar, was thrown into the Vltava in 1393, tied up in a sack. Apparently, he was executed because, as confessor to the Queen, he was privy to unspeakable confidences. Today, statues of St John Nepomuk adorn numerous bridges both in the Czech Republic and in Austria. He was retrieved from obscurity in the 17th century by the Jesuits, who needed a local Catholic saint to help forget the reformist zeal of Jan Hus. They chose a man of the same Christian name who was, like Hus, put to death to be kept quiet. Close to the Malá Strana end of the bridge, you'll see the statue of the knight Bruncvík carrying a sword

and a coat of arms showing a lion, the symbol of his courage. The citizens of the Old Town erected the statue in 1506, in full view of the burghers of Malá Strana, just to show them to whom the bridge and the river really belonged. On top of that they exacted a toll from those crossing the bridge.
The towers at the end of the bridge count among the oldest vestiges in Prague. The left-hand tower was part of the old 12th-century Judith Bridge; that on the right was added in 1464. Its gable ends and ornamentation date from 1591. Down on the right, you can see one of the oldest hotels in Prague: U Tří Pštrosů (The House of the Three Ostriches) which was built during Charles IV's reign.

The Vltava E 1–D 6
Eleven bridges link the two banks of the Vltava (Moldau), the river immortalized in a symphony by the composer Smetana (there is a **Smetana Museum** in the Old Town not far from the Charles Bridge).
The Old Town nestles on the left bank, dominated by the resplendent neo-Renaissance National Theatre. A little further south, the Masaryk quayside boasts several superb Art Nouveau façades (such as the Goethe Institute).

MALÁ STRANA
The Lesser Quarter must be one of the most pleasant districts in Prague for a quiet stroll. Here you'll find the foreign embassies, baroque palaces, peaceful gardens and outdoor restaurants overlooking the Vltava.
 Otakar II founded the Lesser Quarter in 1257 and invited German merchants to settle here. Charles IV later enlarged the district. When Rudolf II of Habsburg (1576–1611) made Prague his capital, he surrounded himself with a glamorous court and invited renowned Italian architects. The nobility and merchants built palaces at the foot of the castle.
 Kampa is a romantic area below Charles Bridge. If you follow Mostecká Street and then, to the left, Lázeňská Street, you reach Malta Square (Maltézské náměstí), home of the Japanese Embassy, and the Turba and Nostic palaces (the latter houses the Dutch Embassy).

Our Lady Beneath the Chain D 3
Kostel Panny Marie Pod Řetězem
Dating from the 12th century, this is the oldest church in Malá Strana, standing on the site of a Romanesque basilica. It belonged to the Knights of Malta.

Velkopřevorské Square D 3
Velkopřevorské náměstí

On the Scene

This tree-shaded square at the end of Lázeňská Street is bordered by the Hrzán Palace (No. 1) with its Renaissance portal, the Buquoy Palace (No. 2), now the French Embassy (with the graffiti-covered "Lennon wall" opposite), and the Palace of the Grand Prior of the Order of Malta (No. 4). If you take Hroznová Street then Na Kampě, you will come to a large park where people come to soak up the sun in summer. Head back along the riverside to pass under the Charles Bridge and roam further along the banks.

Kampa Museum D 3

- U Sovových mlýnů 2
- Daily 10 a.m.–6 p.m.
- Tel. 257 286 147

The old Sova mill on the river bank has been restored to house the Mládek family's collection of modern art. Of particular interest are the sculptures of Otto Gutfreund (1889–1927) and the abstract works of Kupka (1871–1957).

Our Lady of Victory C 3

- Kostel Panny Marie Vítězné
- Karmelitská 9
- Mon–Sat 8.30 a.m.–7 p.m.
- Sun 8.30 a.m.–8 p.m.

Very popular with Italian and Spanish tourists, this church is famous for a small wax figure known as the Holy Infant of Prague, brought from Spain in 1628. It is 46 cm (18 in) high, with a crown of gold encrusted with precious stones, and is greatly revered.
The church acquired its baroque ornamentation from the Spanish Carmelites. Note on many altars paintings in the style of Petr Brandl (1700).

Lesser Quarter Square C 2

- Malostranské náměstí

Heading west along Mostecká Street, you reach the largest square in the Malá Strana quarter, encircling a group of apartment buildings and St Nicholas Cathedral, with an impressive dome and spire.
At No. 21, the former Malá Strana town hall (Malostranská Beseda) now houses, on the first floor, a trendy café and a jazz club popular with young people. The Renaissance house U Splavínů, remodelled in the baroque style in 1720, features a fresco portraying the coronation of the Virgin Mary. Other buildings of great beauty include No. 25, the Kaiserštejn House, dating from the 18th century, and No. 19, the entrance to the Czech National Assembly (along Tomasská Street).
At the upper end of the square, the Liechtenstein Palace (No. 13) is well

known to musicians as the headquarters of the Academy of Music.
The column in the centre of the square was erected in 1715.

St Nicholas Cathedral C 2
- Kostel svatého Mikuláše
- Malostranské náměstí
- March–Oct 9 a.m.–5 p.m., Nov–Feb 9 a.m.–4 p.m.

This cathedral is one of the finest examples of baroque style in Prague. It is the work of the architect Kryštof Dientzenhofer and his son Kilián Ignác Dientzenhofer. Construction began in 1673 on the site of an old Gothic church. Inside, look up at the ceiling, covered with an immense fresco illustrating the life of St Nicholas. Behind the organ, another fresco documents the life of St Cecilia. The fresco in the dome represents the Holy Trinity. The pulpit, from 1765, is particularly handsome.

Wallenstein Palace and Gardens D 2
- Entrance: Valdštejnské náměstí 4 or through the gardens by Letenská 10
- Free admission to some of the palace rooms Sat and Sun 10 a.m.–5 p.m. (enter by interior courtyards). Gardens open daily Apr–Oct 10 a.m.–6 p.m.

Wallenstein Palace is the seat of the Senate and another remarkable example of baroque construction, designed by Italian architects between 1623 and 1630. The gardens (zahrada) are picturesquely laid out with statues (copies of the originals by Adrien de Vries), fountains, geometrical flower beds and peacocks. It makes the perfect setting for a rest before you climb up to the castle. In summer, concerts and plays are staged here in the cool of the evening.

Ledebourg, Palffy, Kolovrat and Fürstenberg Gardens C–D 1
- Entrance: Valdštejnské náměstí 3 or Palffy Palace (Valdštejnské 14)
- Daily Apr, Oct 10 a.m.–6 p.m., May, Sept 10 a.m.–7 p.m., June, July 10 a.m.–9 p.m., Aug 10 a.m.–8 p.m.

Here you may well think you are in Tuscany. These terraced gardens, laid out in the 18th century and recently restored, provide an alternative and attractive route up to the castle, avoiding the streets. Concerts and plays are organized here in summer. These tranquil gardens are one of Prague's little secrets.

Franz Kafka Museum C 3
- Hergetova Cihelna

Cihelna 2b
Tel. 221 451 400
Daily 10 a.m.–6 p.m.
An old brickworks on the riverbank has been restored to make a beautiful modern setting for this museum—a moving and mysterious exploration of Kafka's world, with all first editions of the Prague-born writer's works, letters, diaries, manuscripts, old photographs of the city, drawings and 3-D installations. An excellent way to make acquaintance with the writer and his muses: Dora, Julie, Milena and Felice.
The building also houses a stylish restaurant, the Hergetova Cihelna; from the outdoor terrace you get a splendid view of the river and Charles Bridge.

Vrtba Gardens C 3
Entrance: Karmelitská 25
Apr–Oct daily 10 a.m.–6 p.m.
Designed by F.M. Kanka and recently restored, this park landscaped in baroque style was the grounds of a palace built in 1631. Pass beneath the arch, topped by a sculpture of Hercules (by Matthias Bernard Braun) to see the terraces of greenery affording a superb view over Malá Strana. The splendid *sala terrena* is adorned with murals by Václav Reiner (1669–1743).

Czech Music Museum C 3
Karmelitská 2
Tel. 257 257 777
Daily (except Tues)10 a.m.–6 p.m.
In a former church, hundreds of ancient musical instruments are displayed, together with recordings so you can hear what they sound like.

Nerudova Street B–C 2
This is the main road to the castle. Starting at Lesser Quarter Square, the steep street bears the name of a Czech writer who lived in the House of the Two Suns, No. 47, and the House of the Three Black Eagles, No. 44.
The striking building at No. 5 is the Morzin Palace, now housing the Romanian embassy; while that at No. 20, built 1721–26 by an Italian architect, is the Italian embassy. Some of the apartment buildings have lovely frescoes, but you have to look up to see them: the House of the Three Fiddles, no 12, and the House of the Red Ram, No. 11.

HRADČANY
Northwest of the Vtlava, looming over the city, the Castle district has been considered a separate town since the 9th century. It spreads over 45 ha (112 acres), encompassing the cathedral and its two spires, a basilica, three courtyards, several streets and alleys,

and a number of noteworthy monuments and museums. The castle, the former royal residence, is today the home of the President of the Republic. Its construction retraces the country's history over the centuries from the origins of the Czech nation in 870.

The Castle B–C 1–2
Hradčanské náměstí
Castle esplanade daily Apr– Oct 5 a.m.–midnight;
Nov.–March 6 a.m.–11 p.m.
Changing of the Guard at the castle gates every hour on the hour, 5 a.m.–11 p.m., with fanfare and changing of the flag at noon.
Castle buildings daily
Apr–Oct 9 a.m.–6 p.m.,
Nov–March 9 a.m.–4 p.m.
Closed Dec 24.
Information service in the second and third courtyards.
Two-day entry pass available.
Guided tours daily, except Monday. Audio tape tour and Braille guide.
Tel. 224 373 111
Fax 224 373 300

First Courtyard
The castle entrance is guarded by two awe-inspiring statues of giants engaged in combat, with dagger and bludgeon to despatch their enemies. Emblazoned on the gate's grid is the monogram of Maria Theresa, Empress of Austria. The ceremony of the Changing of the Guard (resplendent in uniforms redesigned by Theodor Pisek, responsible for the costumes in *Amadeus*) is a sight not to be missed. The buildings around this courtyard (1760) are by Niccolo Pacassi. Pass under the Matthias Gate to reach the second courtyard.

Second Courtyard
The buildings and façades of this courtyard, originally 16th century, were modified by Pacassi during the reign of Maria Theresa in the 18th century. To the right, you reach the Chapel of the Holy Cross, built between 1756 and 1763 and containing objects from the cathedral treasury.
In the centre of the square stands a baroque sandstone fountain.
The buildings to the left, the former stables of Ferdinand I and Rudolf II, now house the Castle Gallery. This magnificent collection of Renaissance and baroque paintings includes prestigious works of many old masters, among them Titian and Rubens.
Concerts are held in the exquisite Spanish Hall on the first floor.
If you take the passageway which leads outside the castle, you will see, on the left, a baroque building

On the Scene

It could be a country village, but in fact it is Černínská Street, in the castle district.

that once housed a riding school. To the right is the the Powder Tower where Rudolf II's alchemists conducted their experiments, and further away, the elegant Belvedere pavilion, built in the purest Renaissance style.

Come back to the Second Courtyard. Under the porch giving access to the Third Courtyard and the cathedral, a staircase leads to the offices of the Czech President.

St Vitus's Cathedral
Katedrála Sv. Víta

You have to look up to appreciate this massive cathedral, which fills most of the courtyard. Emperor Charles IV commissioned the French architect Matthias of Arras to start its construction in 1344, on the site of a Romanesque rotunda and basilica. The work was continued by Peter Parler, who added the Late-Gothic touches in the choir vault, the nave and tower. Various events delayed construction: the Hussite wars, a fire in the 15th century, pillage in the 17th. In fact the cathedral was not completed until 1929!

The present entrance under the western, neo-Gothic façade dates from this century. For 500 years, the main entrance was through the Golden Portal on the southern façade. The vaulted roof, supported by 28 pillars, covers three naves 125 m (410 ft) long, 60 m (200 ft) wide and more than 34 m (100 ft) high. Not far from the entrance, on the left, a large stained-glass window designed by Alfons Mucha illustrates the legend of St Methodius. Further on, to the right, the Chapel of St Wenceslas is venerated by the people of Prague. This 14th-century Gothic masterpiece was built on the site where Wenceslas, patron saint of Bohemia, was buried. In the chapel, the statue of the saint bearing a lance dates from 1373. The walls are decorated with 1,345 precious stones. The murals, from the beginning of the 16th century, illustrate the story of St Wenceslas. Pursued by his brother Boleslav, he managed to grasp the bronze lion's-head doorknocker as he sought sanctuary, but did not make it inside, and was slain by his brother's sword.

A stairway leads to the Royal Treasury, locked in by no less than seven keys. The crown jewels of Bohemia are kept here, including a sword, the crown, sceptre, orb, mantle and stoles.

As you look around the cathedral, you can't miss St John Nepomuk's extravagant tomb, fashioned in 1733–36 from two tonnes of silver and festooned with candle-bearing cherubs.

The cathedral pulpit is in Renaissance style. In front of the neo-Gothic high altar, an imposing mausoleum contains the remains of Emperor Ferdinand I of Habsburg, his wife, and their son Maximilian. From the Chapel of the Holy Cross, a stairway leads to the royal crypt containing the tombs of Charles IV, his four wives, and their children. The Chapel of Saxony and Chapel of Our Lady, containing Gothic tombs, are closer to the choir.

Climb the stairs to the top of the cathedral tower. It's hard going, but well worth the effort for the sweeping view of Prague.

Once outside the cathedral, turn to the right to admire the Golden Portal, crowned by a superb 14th-century mosaic and decorated with figures of the kings of Bohemia and of Charles IV and his wife.

A bit further on, you reach the Mihulka Powder Tower where Rudolf II's alchemists used to carry out their experiments (visit the exhibition).

Old Royal Palace
Starý Královský palác

This building, located at the further end of the Third Courtyard, was the

On the Scene

residence of the Bohemian princes up to the 16th century. The magnificent Vladislav Hall was begun in 1493 by Benedikt Ried, who was knighted for the achievement. With a length of 62 m (200 ft), it is the largest vaulted hall of Europe in Flamboyant Gothic style. Jousting tournaments and banquets were once held here, and the staircase you take was originally designed for horses. From Vladislav Hall, you can reach the Renaissance-style Louis Palace, named after Louis Jaguellon, son of Vladislav, on the right, then, to the left, the old Diet Hall where the kings were elected. Newly elected presidents take the oath here, as prescribed in the Constitution. After seeing the Chapel of All Saints, take the Knights' Staircase to reach the Gothic palace, which houses an exhibition on the castle's history.

St George's Basilica
- Basilika sv. Jiří

The square behind the cathedral was the castle's central square in the Middle Ages. Facing you is the baroque façade of the basilica. The interior of the church, with three naves and two towers, is Romanesque. Don't miss the beautiful 12th-century paintings and various tombs.

St George's Convent
- Klášter sv. Jiří
- Daily (except Mon)
- 10 a.m.–6 p.m.

Adjoining the basilica, the convent of the same name, founded in 973, is believed to be the oldest building in Bohemia. Here, you can discover a National Gallery collection of 19th-century artworks by Czech artists, including paintings, sculpture and decorative arts.

Golden Lane
- Zlatá ulička
- Entry fee included in the Prague Castle short route ticket

From St George's Square, take Jiřská Street, then, on the left, the passageway U Daliborky to reach picturesque Golden Lane. Legend relates that Rudolf II installed alchemists' laboratories and workshops here to manufacture gold (thence the name). In fact, this little street was originally inhabited by the gunners of the royal guard. Later, people of modest means found a home here. Franz Kafka's sister lodged at No. 22, and the writer stayed with her for several months. The pretty houses with tiled roofs and pastel-painted walls now mostly contain boutiques and souvenir shops.

At either end of the lane, the White Tower and Daliborka Tower form

On the Scene

part of the castle fortifications and served as prisons.

Toy Museum
- Muzeum Hraček
- Jiřská 6
- Daily 9.30 a.m.–5.30 p.m.

An amazing display of toys of every period from antiquity onwards, including a collection of Barbie dolls. But parents may enjoy it more than the kids as everything is kept safely out of reach in glass cases.

Castle Square B 2
- Hradčanské náměstí

Fringed with large buildings, this square has at its centre the Plague Column, which commemorates the end of the fearsome epidemic of 1679. At No. 15, a passageway takes you to the Sternberg Palace.

Sternberg Palace B 2
- Štenberský palác
- Hradčanské náměstí 1
- Daily (except Mon) 10 a.m.–6 p.m.
- Tel. 220 514 634

The palace houses the impressive National Gallery collections of European art, with works of the German, Austrian, Dutch and Italian schools, including masterpieces by Dürer, Rembrandt, Rubens, El Greco and Goya. This is the largest collection of Old Masters to be seen in Prague.

Schwarzenberg Palace B 2
- Schwarzenberský palác
- Hradčanské náměstí 2
- Daily (except Mon)
- 10 a.m.–6 p.m.

The Schwarzenberg Palace is one of the rare Renaissance palaces in Prague, and one of the most impressive. The façades are adorbed with superb diamond-point sgraffito work. The palace is the setting of a remarkable exhibition, Mannerism and Baroque in Bohemia, displaying statues and paintings from the collections of the National Gallery, notably 15 works by Karel Škréta (1610–1674) including a beautiful Birth of the Virgin.

Loretánské Square B 2
- Loretánské náměstí

Going down Loretánská from the top of Castle Square, you reach this square built between 1703 and 1726. At No. 1, the façade of the beer house U Černého Vola (The Black Ox) features a fresco of St Luke, patron saint of artists, who is shown painting an elegant Madonna and Child. At No. 5, the imposing Černín Palace, the largest baroque palace in Prague, designed by Italian architects, is today the headquarters of the Ministry of Foreign Affairs. Beyond it you can glimpse the spires of the Loreto church.

On the Scene

Our Lady of Loreto A 2

Loreta
Loretánské náměstí 7
Daily (except Mon)
9 a.m.–12.15 p.m., 1–4.30 p.m.

This church was built between 1626 and 1750 in honour of Loreto, a well-known place of pilgrimage in Italy where angels are said to have transported the Santa Casa, the Nazareth house where Jesus and the Virgin Mary once lived.

Try to be there on the hour, when the church's carillon of 27 bells chime a hymn.

Go under the porch to the courtyard where two baroque fountains play, one on each side of a square building which is the sculpted and stuccoed replica of the Santa Casa. Inside is a series of paintings relating the life of the Virgin Mary, a silver altar, and a carved wooden Madonna.

The courtyard is surrounded by cloisters on two levels, of which the lower one was reserved for pilgrims. The ground-floor gallery is bordered by 22 altars and 7 chapels. One of these is dedicated to a Spanish saint sporting a beard, which would not seem unusual, except that it happens to be a woman. After begging God to spare her from an arranged marriage, she miraculously sprouted a beard to discourage the suitor.

On the first floor of the cloisters, the Loreto Treasury contains more than 300 religious objects from the 16th to 18th centuries, including candlesticks, chalices and monstrances. The most remarkable exhibit is a diamond-studded monstrance made in Vienna in the 17th century: 89.5 cm (35 in) high and weighing 12 kilos (26 lb), it represents a sun with rays fashioned out of 6,200 diamonds. Everything is well labeled in English as well as Czech.

End your tour by visiting the Nativity Church, built between 1734 and 1737, to admire the striking fresco on the ceiling, depicting the presentation of Jesus in the Temple.

Nový Svět Street A 1

This is probably one of the most picturesque walks to be enjoyed in Prague. If you need a bit of respite after a tiring visit to the castle, it provides a welcome change of scenery.

From the Loreto, take the steep, cobbled Černínská Street on the right, passing villas surrounded by peaceful greenery. Then turn right into Nový Svět, a narrow, winding street that takes you past an excellent restaurant, U Zlaté Hrušky, at No. 3. Bear right again onto Kanovnická, which leads down to the Castle Square.

On the Scene

Strahov Monastery A 3
- Strahovský klášter
- Strahovské nádvoří 1/132
- Daily (except Mon)
- 9 a.m.–noon, 1.30–5 p.m.

Walk due west of the Loreto to Pohořelec Square. From No. 8, a narrow stairway climbs to the courtyard of the superb Strahov monastery. The main entrance is a bit further up.

Established in 1143 by the Order of Premonstratensians, the monastery was transformed into a museum in 1952, but it was returned to the monks only a few years ago. Apart from the attractive façades of the churches of St Roch and Our Lady, the monastery is especially known for its splendid 12th-century library, made up of more than 130,000 books, 25,000 manuscripts and 2,000 incunabula. The Theological Hall is redolent of history and erudition. It was designed by an Italian architect in 1671 especially to store religious books. Ceiling frescoes painted by one of the monks in 1727 are a symbolic celebration of books. Notice the globes showing the world as it was known in the 17th century. The 32-m (144-ft) Philosophical Hall contains over 50,000 works on philosophy and history, beneath a ceiling fresco illustrating the story of mankind. Beyond the monastery courtyard, you can enjoy a fantastic view over the city of Prague, with the castle to the left and Malá Strana spreading below. Úvoz Street takes you back to Malá Strana.

Petřín Hill Observation Tower B 3
- Petřínská Rozhledna
- Daily Apr, Sept, Oct
- 10 a.m.–7 p.m.,
- May–Aug 10 a.m.–10 p.m.,
- Dec 10 a.m.–6 p.m.
- Sat, Sun only Nov, Jan–March
- 10 a.m.–6 p.m.

Behind the entrance to the Strahov monastery, a winding path through wooded groves on Petřín hill leads to the 60-m (200-ft) Observation Tower, a replica of the Eiffel Tower erected in 1891 as part of an exhibition. For a wide-angle view of Prague, climb the 299 steps to the top of the tower, which has the unnerving habit of swaying slightly in a strong wind. From Petřín, you can return to Malá Strana by cable car (operates 9.15 a.m.–8.45 p.m.).

OTHER MONUMENTS

Vyšehrad Castle
- Praha 2
- Soběslavova 1
- Metro Line C to Vyšehradská station

On the Scene

According to old Czech legends, the first princes of Bohemia dwelt here on top of a rocky outcrop. In the 11th century, Prince Vratislav II built a Romanesque palace and several churches. Later, Emperor Charles IV contributed a royal palace. Vyšehrad eventually developed into a fortress, which was destroyed in 1866. Head for St Martin's rotunda, the oldest part of Vyšehrad (11th century). Originally Romanesque, the Basilica of Sts Peter and Paul was reconstructed in Gothic style during Emperor Charles IV's reign. Among the illustrious personages in Vyšehrad cemetery are composers Smetana and Dvořák and writers Jan Neruda and Karel Čapek.

Mozart Museum, Villa Bertramka

Museum W.A. Mozarta
Mozartova 169, Smichov, Praha 5
Metro Line B to Anděl station
Tel. 257 318 461
Daily Apr–Oct 9 a.m.–6 p.m.,
Nov–March 9.30 a.m.–4 p.m.

This elegant villa was the home of Czech composer and pianist František Xaver Dušek and his wife, Josefína Duskova. Mozart was a frequent guest and it was here, in 1787, that he composed the opera, *Don Giovanni*. The museum contains his white harpsichord and a grand piano. For concerts see p. 38.

Trade Fair Palace

Veletržní palác
Praha 7
Dukelských hrdinů 7
Tram 12 or 17
Tel. 24 30 11 11
Daily (except Mon) 10 a.m.–6 p.m.

The 8-storey building, dating from 1925, is a gigantic art gallery. The 2nd floor is devoted to Czech art from 1930 to the present day, while early 20th-century works are displayed on the 3rd floor, along with 19th–20th century French art (Maillol, Rousseau, Braque, Picasso, and more). The Czech Romantic school of the 19th century is represented on the 4th floor.

Dvořák Museum

Dvořákovo Muzeum
Ke Karlovu 20
Metro Line C to IP Pavlova station
Daily (except Mon)
Apr–Sept 10 a.m.–1.30 p.m.,
2–5.30 p.m., Oct–March
9.30 a.m.–1.30 p.m., 2–5 p.m.

The museum is housed in the 18th-century baroque Villa Amerika, by Kilián Ignác Dienzenhofer. It displays the composer's original scores, his quill, letters, photographs and personal belongings, including the cap and gown he wore when he received an honorary doctorate from Cambridge University in 1891.

Entertainment

As evening falls, the street lamps fill Prague with a warm, golden light, conducive to mystery and poetry. The palaces of Malá Strana, the baroque churches, the theatres and the concert halls come alive with music and song. The Czechs love dressing up to go to a concert or show. For a long time, under the communist regime, music was their only means of expressing themselves freely.

Programmes for the various performances are distributed in the streets some hours in advance. Concerts and operas usually start around 7 p.m.

THEATRE

In Prague, three great theatres stand out especially for their superb architecture, which puts the audience in a suitably festive mood even before the curtain rises.

National Theatre E 4
Národní divadlo
Ostrovni 1
Tel. 224 913 437
Opera, ballet and drama are staged here.

Entertainment

State Opera
Státní Opera Praha
Legerova 75
Tel. 296 117 111
Marvellous performances of opera and ballet.

Estates Theatre
Stavovské divadlo
Ovocný trh 1
Tel. 224 901 448
Called the Tyl Theatre from 1945 to 1991, it now stages excellent ballet and opera performances—just the place to enjoy an opera by Mozart: the composer directed the first performance of *Don Giovanni* in this cosy little theatre in the heart of the Old Town.

OTHER VENUES

Rudolfinum E 2
Alšovo nábřeží 12
Tel. 227 059 227
A neo-Renaissance building constructed between 1876 and 1884, headquarters of the Czech Philharmonic Orchestra. The Dvořák hall is famous for its concerts staged during the Prague Spring music festival.

Laterna Magika F 4
Nová Scéna National Theatre
Národní 4
Tel. 224 931 482/222 222 041

> **TICKETS**
> To find out what's on during your stay, and to buy tickets, contact one of the following companies:
>
> Bohemia Ticket
> Malé námešti 13
> tel. 224 227 832
> fax 224 219 480
> Mon–Fri 9 a.m.–5 p.m.,
> Sat 9 a.m.–1 p.m.
> www.bohemiaticket.cz
> order@bohemiaticket.cz
>
> Čedok, Na Příkopě 18
> tel. 224 197 642
> Mon–Fri 9 a.m.–7 p.m.
> Sat, Sun 9.30 a.m.–1 p.m.
> Excellent information, guided tours and bookings.

A large and popular theatre proposing a unique kind of drama. The show at the "Magic Lantern" combines film backdrop on multi-screens with live ballet performance, and will enchant you with its poetic atmosphere.

National Marionette Theatre
Žatecká 1
Old Town
Tickets and information daily 10 a.m.–8 p.m.
Tel. 224 819 322
This isn't just kid's stuff. Behind the curtain and the colourful stage sets, the puppeteers wielding the

wooden characters—which can weigh up to 7 kg—are professional actors. The tradition dates back to the 17th century: when German was imposed as the official language, puppets were allowed to continue "speaking" Czech—a valuable way of preserving local culture. The performance of *Don Giovanni* is a saucy if irreverent look at Mozart's opera. You can't help but join in the laughter.

Bertramka – Muzeum W.A. Mozarta
- "Original Music Theatre Prague"
- Villa Bertramka
- Mozartova 169
- Praha 5
- Tel. 257 318 461

Mozart visited Prague several times an met with considerable success, a refreshing change from the mockery he had to endure in Salzburg, his home town. When he conducted the premiere of *Don Giovanni* in the Estates Theatre in 1787, Mozart was the guest of Dušeks, who provided these bucolic surroundings where he could compose in peace. Today, musical evenings (champagne included) are organized in the villa, some distance from the centre of Prague. Mozart's works are performed by actors and singers in superb period costumes.

CLUBS
A trendy atmosphere prevails in the following nightspots:

U Malého Glena
- Karmelitská 23
- Malá Strana
- Tel. 257 531 717

A popular gathering place for the locals, who spend their evenings in the cellars of this restaurant in a rustic setting. Jazz and blues groups from 9.30 p.m.

Radost FX
- Bělehradská 120
- Open 9 p.m.–5 a.m.
- Tel. 224 254 776

This place is divided into several areas. You can dine, or just have a coffee or a drink in a cool atmosphere. Dancefloor in the basement, with techno music.

Reduta
- Národní 20
- Every night 9.30 p.m.–midnight
- Tel. 224 933 487

For jazz lovers.

Agharta Jazz Centrum
- Železná 16
- Open 3 p.m.–midnight
- Tel. 222 211 275
- Open evenings 6 p.m.–1 a.m.

Laid-back atmosphere, very popular with the locals.

Dining Out

The expansive girth of many Prague citizens is ample proof of the richness of the local cuisine: heavy sauces, calorie-loaded pastries, plenty of beer… You may as well put your diet on hold while you're in Prague. If you don't want to spend too much, get away from the city centre and dine in one of the smaller restaurants, often serving good food in copious helpings. In the more touristy areas the bill can be much higher, but prices still compare well with those practised in other European capitals. To give you an idea of prices, $ = under 150 Kč; $$ = from 150 to 500 Kč; $$$ over 500 Kč.

NOVÉ MĚSTO

La Perle de Prague
Tančící dům (Dancing House)
Rašínovo nábřeží 80
Tel. 221 984 160

Prague's best restaurant occupies a lofty position on the 7th floor of Frank Gehry's famously contorted building known as the Dancing House. The atmosphere is hushed and elegant, the cuisine typical of

Dining Out

the south of France, lovingly prepared by a talented chef. Impressive view of the castle. $$$

Le Louvre
- Národní 20
- Daily 8 a.m.–11 p.m.

Traditional café decorated with stucco. The clientèle is a strange mix: young people who come to spend hours over their newspapers, and old ladies who meet up for a good gossip. Billiards room open in the afternoons. $

Novoměstský Pivovar
- Vodičkova 20

The good people of Prague love to meet in this beer house, a veritable maze of rooms decorated with old-fashioned murals. You can see the actual brewing vats. It's located on a side street off Wenceslas Square. Typical cuisine, reasonable prices. $$

Slavia
- Smetanovo nábřeži 2
- Daily 8 a.m.–11 p.m.

This was long the haunt of intellectuals and actors, and it was here that President Havel met his first wife Olga. A good place for a quick lunch, with a view of the banks of the Vltava. The restaurant at the front offers very inexpensive dishes in a pleasant setting. $

U Fleků
- Křemencova 11
- Tel. 224 934 019

CAFÉS AND BEER HOUSES

The cafés *(kavárna)* where local intellectuals used to exchange ideas in the early 20th century have almost all disappeared. The legendary Slavia (opposite the National Theatre) has just been opened after seemingly endless years of renovation. You can also sip a Turkish coffee or an expresso at the Savoy, founded in 1877. The ceilings are superb.

If beer is your tipple you would be well advised to venture into a *pivnice* (beer house). There's plenty going on in these noisy, smoke-filled establishments, and the sight of the waiters laden with overflowing jars, nimbly dancing from one table to the other, is fascinating.

If you ask for a *pivo* you will be served half a litre, around a pint. If that seems a bit excessive, try a *malé pivo* (small beer), about a third of a litre, just over half a pint.

The Czechs have an infallible method for testing their beer for quality: if you place a 10-halířů coin on the foam, you should be able to count to ten before it sinks.

Dining Out

A venerable beer house, which has been serving a dark beer since 1499. It has six 16th-century vaulted rooms, and quiet gardens for summer drinking.

STARÉ MĚSTO

Allegro
- Veleslavínova 2A/1098
- Daily 11.30 a.m.–10.30 p.m.
- Tel. 221 426 880

This was the first restaurant in the Czech Republic to win a Michelin star (2008). The chef Andrea Accordi presides over the Four Seasons restaurant inventing refined dishes of Italian inspiration. Several sampling menus and impressive wine cellar. Air conditioned, impeccable service. $$$

Bakeshop Praha
- Kozí 1
- Tel. 222 316 823

Do not miss this bakery if you want to make a good, light lunch. Deliciously crusty bread, a wide variety of quiches and salads, imaginative sandwiches, not to mention cakes and brownies. For eating on the spot or takeaway. $

Bellevue
- Smetanovo nábřeží 18
- Lunch noon–3 p.m.,
- dinner 5.30–11 p.m.
- Brunch-jazz Sun 11 a.m.–3 p.m.
- Tel. 222 221 443

Excellent and hearty cuisine, for example saddle of venison with cranberries and mushrooms. Good view of the castle. $$$

Blatnička
- Michalská 6–8
- Daily 11 a.m.–11 p.m.

A varied menu in English and Czech, offering reasonably priced specialities. Rustic décor, efficient service, and a friendly clientèle comprised mainly of locals. $

Brasserie La Provence
- Štupartská 9
- Tel. 296 826 155

If it's cold outside, the Parisian Belle-Epoque décor of La Provence bar/restaurant will soon transport you to sunnier climes. Comfy sofas, cosy atmosphere and heartwarming cuisine, including large platters of seafood. $$$

Chez Marcel
- Haštalské 12
- Tel. 222 315 676

For a change from Czech fare, you might like to try this French bistro. The décor is reasonably authentic, and the steaks are thick, tender and delicious, served with gratin dauphinois. Also duck fillet with green pepper, rabbit with basil. $$

Dining Out

Grand Café Praha
Staroměstské náměstí 22
7 a.m.–10 p.m.
In the building opposite the astronomical clock, on the first floor. Besides delicious pastries, the café offers a ring-side seat for observing the activity in the Square. $

Havelská Koruna
Havelská 21
Daily 9 a.m.–8 p.m.
For those who have to stick to a tight budget, this café and self-service restaurant is well worth a visit. Rustic décor, wide variety of inexpensive dishes. You can just call in for cakes and a cup of excellent coffee. $

Nostress
Dušni 10
Restaurant daily
10 a.m.–midnight
Gallery daily noon–10 p.m.
Tel. 222 317 007
Restaurant and gallery situated just opposite the Spanish Synagogue. Minimalist décor, where the furniture and modern works of art are almost all for sale. Relaxing music, refined cuisine. Try the chicken in satay sauce. $$

Obecní Dům
Náměstí Republiky 5
7.30 a.m.–11 p.m.
Located in the Municipal House, next to the Powder Gate. Recently renovated, this is one of the few surviving intellectuals' cafés. The Art Nouveau décor is superb. $

U Prince
Staroměstské náměstí 29
Tel. 224 213 807
Opposite the astronomical clock. Wonderful old-fashioned decor in vaulted dining rooms, and extremely good cuisine. Try the venison salad with olives, the Parma ham with horseradish, or the grilled duck. Reasonable prices. $$

U Zlatého Tygra
Husova 17
Typical Czech tavern, between the Old Town Square and Charles Bridge. Very few tourists ever venture into this establishment, which is another rendez-vous of Prague's intellectuals. Highbrow and smoky atmosphere guaranteed. The vaulted room dates from the 13th century. Try the strong-smelling "beer cheese", served with bread. $

MALÁ STRANA

C'est la vie
Řični 1
Tel. 721 158 403
A popular address; plain and classy décor for this restaurant where the

client is well looked after. Only a few tables inside; in summer sit outside beside the river. Good choice of fish. $$$

Palffy Palác
Valdštejnské 14
11 a.m.–11 p.m.
Tel./fax 257 530 522
On the first floor of a magnificent 18th-century palace, which also houses the Conservatory of Music, this restaurant has an elegant stuccoed dining room with a high ceiling. Excellent cuisine, to be enjoyed to music and in candlelight. $$$

U Modré Kachničky
Nebovidská 6
Noon–4 p.m., 6.30–midnight
Tel. 257 320 308
Counts among one of the best restaurants of the town, in a quiet street. Intimate atmosphere; Art nouveau furnishings. Try the carp

THE TASTE OF PRAGUE

Czech delis are veritable monuments to the glory of the pig: festooned in sausages and saveloys, bolonies, hams and various other cooked meats. The smell can be overpowering. In Prague the sausage reigns supreme.

Apart from the traditional grilled sausages served with mild mustard on a slice of bread at the stands on Wenceslas Square, there are other specialities worth seeking out when you want more than a snack. When you decipher the restaurant menus, you'll see *pečená kachna* (grilled duck) or *husa* (goose). There's also venison with cranberries and cream *(srnčí)* and pork, smoked or otherwise, often in breadcrumbs and fried *(smažený řízek)*. Hearty eaters might like to tackle *koleno* (pig's knuckles) served with mild mustard or black radish. Vegetarians are in trouble, but they can always fall back on fish or *smažený sýr* (deep-fried cheese).

It isn't worth ordering several courses; this is not dainty nouvelle cuisine. Usually, a serving fills up the whole plate. Pork is often accompanied by a generous helping of sweetish sauerkraut, with the inevitable bread dumplings called *knedlíky*. You could do worse than order the carp in breadcrumbs *(kapr)*, a traditional Christmas dish.

If you have a sweet tooth you'll be spoiled for choice. The *zákusky* (cream cakes) are irresistible, as are the *palačinky*, pancakes filled with whipped cream, fruit and ice cream, sometimes flambéed. Another tempting possibility is the classic *štrůdl*.

As they say in Prague, *Dobrou chuť*—enjoy your meal!

with cumin or pheasant in spicy sauce. $$$

U Malířů
Maltézské náměstí 11
Tel. 257 530 000
This is arguably the best restaurant in Prague, with a good menu offering the best of classic French cuisine. The setting is charming, all vaulted ceilings and old murals, and subdued lighting for an intimate atmosphere. Restricted number of tables. The menu is impressive—quail in Armagnac, foie gras, lobster—with prices to match. $$$

> **THE BEST BEER**
> Beer is the Czech national drink. The secret of its flavour lies in the quality of the hops, grown in northern Bohemia, and of the water and malt used. According to the ancient chronicles, hops were grown in Bohemia back in the 9th century. The beer trade was considered so important that the king of Bohemia himself granted the licence for brewing it. In the 16th century, beer was spiced up with nutmeg, bay and juniper berries.
> Among the various types of beer on offer today, try the light Staropramen or Gambrinus (a Pilsener), both appreciated for their bitter taste. Budvar is somewhat milder. *Světlé pivo* is light beer, and *černé pivo* is dark.

U Mecenáše
Malostranské náměstí 10
Noon–11.30 p.m.
Tel. 257 531 631
A typical restaurant in a 16th-century house, with two dining rooms in the traditional style. $$$

U Tomáše
Letenská 12
This is the oldest beer house in Prague, providing liquid refreshment since 1358! There's a fine medieval cellar. A dark beer is brewed on the premises. Live music in the evenings. $$

HRADČANY

Hanavský Pavilon
Letenské sady 173
Tel. 233 323 641
A little baroque palace up above the city, offering a superb view over the Vltava river and the Old Town. $$$

Lobkowicz Café
Jiřská 3
Tel. 602 595 998
An elegant café in the Lobkowicz Palace (just follow the red carpet from the Toy Museum). Light cuisine, or just coffee and cakes. Enjoy the delicately painted dining rooms or sit outside on the terrace: terrific view! $$

Shopping

Apart from shops specializing in glittering crystal and appealing souvenirs, Prague has several attractive fashion boutiques, some of them housed in palaces, and there are plenty of antique shops, where prices tend to be high.

In general, shops are open Monday to Friday 9 a.m. to 6 p.m., and some close an hour for lunch. The larger stores stay open until 8 p.m.

FOOD

Supermarkets in the centre of Prague are as well stocked as those of other European cities, with a wide range of products. If you need a few picnic items, you can go to one of the many neighbourhood *potraviny* (grocery shops). For the sweet-toothed, there are plenty of *cukrárna* (pastry shops).

Tesco

Národni 26
Mon–Fri 8 a.m.–9 p.m.,
Sat 9 a.m.– 8 p.m.,
Sun 10 a.m.–7p.m.

The inhabitants of Prague adore Tesco, which has spread over four floors right in the middle of town. You can find everything you need, and there's a good food department in the basement.

FASHION AND ACCESSORIES

Top boutiques and stores, many of them with a futuristic design, are on a par with the best in Europe. Well-known brands in fashion, perfumes, shoes and so on are available.

Bata
- Václavské náměsti 6
- Mon–Fri 9 a.m.–9 p.m.,
- Sat 9 a.m.–8 p.m.,
- Sun 10 am.–8 p.m.

Shoe heaven! Seven floors of shoes of every kind imaginable, at reasonable prices.

Model
- Václavské náměsti 28
- Mon–Fri 9 a.m.–7 p.m.;
- Sat 10 a.m.–6 p.m.
- Sun 10 a.m.–5 p.m.

If you suddenly find you need a hat for a wedding, or just to keep your ears warm, call in here. Attractive designs, and prices so reasonable you might as well buy two.

Nový Smíchov
- Plzeňska 8
- Metro Anděl
- Daily 7 a.m.–midnight

In the modern district of Anděl, not far from the historic centre, this new shopping centre is the most popular in town. Grandiose futuristic architecture and a great number of boutiques, restaurants and cinemas.

Pasáž Myslbek – Nákupní Gallery
- Na Příkopě 19/21

Shopping centre located at the bottom of Wenceslas Square, full of sparkling new boutiques.

GIFTS

Prague isn't the ideal place for buying antiques as prices in the city centre are prohibitive. Furthermore, you need special permission to take antiques out of the country; export of religious objects is forbidden. If you want to buy presents for your friends at home, you could settle on a bottle or two of Becherovka liqueur, which tastes a bit like Chartreuse, or you could consider crystal or puppets.

Alma starozitnosti
- Valentinska 7

This antique shop in the Old Town has a treasure-trove of 1920s to 1940s costume jewellery, retrieved from Bohemian factories closed during communist rule.

Antik Mucha
- Liliova 12
- Mon–Sat 10 a.m.–6 p.m.
- Tel. 222 221 523

Shopping

Cupboards overflowing with genuine Art Nouveau and Belle-Epoque jewellery, and Cubist lamps and decorative items from the 1950s dotted here and there—this antique shop near Charles Bridge is a wonderful place for browsing and filling your bags with souvenirs.

Botanicus
Ungelt Týn 1049

Perfumes, essential oils, dried flowers, soap and other fragrant cosmetics based on organic cultivation in a beautifully fitted shop in natural wood. Traditional hand-made products.

Český Národní Podnik
Melantrichova 17
Karlova 26
Nerudova 31
Železná 3

These shops in the city centre offer handcrafted wood items, decorated Easter eggs and so on.

Kotva
Náměstí Republiky 8
Mon–Fri 9 a.m.–8 p.m.,
Sat 10 a.m.–7 p.m.,
Sun 10 a.m.–6 p.m.

You'll find just about everything here; crystal is a good buy.

Moser
Na Příkopě 12
Mon–Fri 10 a.m.–8 p.m.,
Sat, Sun 10 a.m.–7 p.m.
Tel. 224 211 293

A good address for Moser crystal, in a fairytale setting. It's very fragile but refined and superbly crafted.

Sklo Bohemia
Na Příkopě 17
Mon–Sat 9 a.m.– 7.30 p.m.
Tel. 224 210 574

A huge range of Bohemia brand glass, cut, etched and coloured. The lead content contributes to solidity.

PUPPETS

The Czechs have been very fond of puppets since the days when German was imposed as the official language, and only marionettes had the right to express themselves in Czech. Today, string, glove and rod puppets are sold in countless shops and stalls in the centre of Prague. Before you buy, compare prices and the materials used: wood, plaster, china. Among the characters dearest to the Czechs are Kašpárek, an amiable clown dressed in red, and Honza, the simple country lad who, thanks to his common sense, saved a princess from being devoured by a dragon and ended up by marrying her. Not forgetting the Good Soldier Švejk with his cap and somewhat naive expression.

Excursions

The Czech Republic is made up of two regions—Bohemia in the west and Moravia in the east. It is said to be the European country with the largest number of castles per inhabitant. Take time to explore the countryside, away from the main roads and the big cities. Travelling through dense forests of fir trees, you will suddenly stumble upon a fortress, a Renaissance castle or the colourful main square in a small provincial town.

BOHEMIA

If all that hearty Czech food is proving to be more than your system can take, a stay in one of the spa towns, Karlovy Vary, Marienbad or Františkovy Lázně, may be just what the doctor ordered. All three boast a privileged setting for hydrotherapy cures.

These towns used to be a favourite gathering place for the aristocracy. Later they were popular with *maminkas* (as the Czechs affectionately call their mothers), who could enjoy cures free of charge under the communist regime. After the Velvet Revolution, the spa buildings were restored to offer once again the

Excursions

healthy benefits of natural springs in a refined environment.

Many famous people have frequented these havens of peace: Bismarck, Brahms, Chopin, Chateaubriand, Freud, Marx, Tolstoy and many others. One of the most loyal clients was Goethe, a great believer in hydrotherapy, who met here the last great love of his life, Ulrike von Levetzov, 55 years his junior.

Karlovy Vary

- 118 km (73 miles) west of Prague

The town is very popular with German visitors seeking relief from their ailments. The stylized buildings date from the 17th, 18th and 19th centuries. The thermal springs, approved in 1358 by Charles IV, total a dozen and their waters are endowed with medicinal qualities for treating back pains, obesity, and high blood pressure.

Few pleasures can beat a stroll through the landscaped gardens, beneath the Mill Colonnade, an elegant neoclassical construction, or the more modern Spring Colonnade, where the healing waters gush forth. Regular concerts are held to entertain the water-drinkers, who are all equipped with a *kalíšek*, a spouted porcelain cup (you can buy one if you want an unusual souvenir).

The town of Karlovy Vary stands on several hills in the middle of a forest. Visit the splendid Russian Orthodox church, the Grand Hotel Pupp and the Baths where you can soak in the same tub as the illustrious emperor Francis Joseph. High above the town, hidden among the firs, the Imperial Hotel looks like an impregnable citadel. The Soviet leaders used to gather here for opulent partying; Brezhnev had his own suite.

Mariánské Lázně

Verdant Marienbad looks as if it were built on a golf course. The architecture is similar to that of Karlovy Vary, including an elegant colonnade built in 1889, next to the more modern "singing" fountain.

Františkovy Lázně

Founded in 1791, this is a true haven of peace, with 25 thermal springs, well-maintained parks and gardens, and bandstands.

Cheb

Not far from Františkovy Lázně, on the border with Bavaria, the little town of Cheb takes you into the past, with its medieval marketplace and town hall, its 13th-century timber-frame houses that belonged to Jewish merchants, its Gothic churches and its castle.

Excursions

Tábor

88 km (55 miles) south of Prague Tábor was built as a fortress by Jan Žižka, a Hussite commander, with the streets laid out in a maze to confuse invaders. The religious and political movement split into two factions in the 15th century, and Tábor was the headquarters of the more militant Taborite group. The museum in the Gothic town hall is devoted to the Hussite movement. The Transfiguration Church, the Augustinian church and the Kotnov castle are also of architectural interest.

Jindřichův Hradec

South of Tábor, Jindřichův Hradec has a lovely triangular square bordered by Renaissance, baroque and classical buildings. A quick tour of the town should include the Trinity column (1764), the castle at the edge of the carp-filled pond, and the old beer house.

Červená Lhota

Between Tábor and Jindřichův Hradec, the castle of Červená Lhota is a Renaissance manor surrounded by a pond which mirrors the castle's bright red walls, a delightful sight.

České Budějovice

The arcaded square of this city of 95,000 is said to be the largest in Bohemia. Each side measures 130 m (425 ft), utterly charming and harmonious, bordered by Gothic, baroque and Renaissance buildings and listed as a historical monument. You can tour the square in an open carriage.

Hluboká nad Vltavou

With its eleven towers and its bastions standing proudly on a rocky hill, the castle of Hluboká nad Vltavou, 10 km (6 miles) north of České Budějovice, seems to have come straight out of a fairy tale. This fortress was built between 1840 and 1881, in the English Windsor style. Worth a visit for its wood panelling, tapestry and the library, holding some 12,000 volumes.

Český Krumlov

Further south, the town of Český Krumlov, founded in the 12th century, nestles on the banks of the Vltava river. There are 250 monuments of interest here. The castle, the second-largest in the country after Prague's, dates back to the 13th century. It was later adapted to the Renaissance style. Visit the hall of masks and the baroque theatre.

Karlštejn Castle

28 km (17 miles) south of Prague

Excursions

Surrounded by forested hills, this castle is the work of the French architect Matthias of Arras at the request of Charles IV, built 1348–57. Its purpose was to store the royal and imperial crown jewels. The latter were moved to Prague Castle in 1625. The exhibition in the Courtesans Hall traces the history of Karlštejn, while the Luxembourg Hall features the busts of Charles IV's family. Do not miss the Chapel of St Catherine, the walls of which are covered in precious stones.

Konopiště
- 40 km (25 miles) southeast of Prague

The castle of Konopiště, was built in the 12th century, and then rebuilt in the late-Gothic style, with further Renaissance additions. It is famous for its large park and the arms and armour collection of the Austrian Archduke Franz Ferdinand, who was a passionate hunter and would shoot anything with fur or feathers. His murder in Sarajevo in 1914 sparked off World War I.

Kutná Hora
- 65 km (40 miles) southeast of Prague

This medieval town is famous for its silver mines, which operated between the 12th and 18th centuries. Through the courtyard of the Vlašský dvůr (Italian Court), you reach the museum which includes the workshops where coins were minted. The superb Gothic Cathedral of St Barbara, the patron saint of miners, is one of the most outstanding in Bohemia. Begun in 1388 to plans by Peter Parler, the project was later completed by Benedikt Rieth and Matthias Rejsek. The macabre Sedlec Chapel, 3 km (2 miles) northwest of the main square, was built in the 12th century and decorated with the bones of 10,000 dead.

Kuks Castle
Kuks is worth the detour for its open-air museum of baroque art. Having won fame and fortune in the wars, Count Franz Anton Špork commissioned an Italian architect to design an original setting in which to entertain his glittering court. Built between 1694 and 1724, Kuks was a combination of castle and spa town. All you can visit from this dazzling period are the hospice and the fabulous Pharmacy Hall. But it is worth coming just to see the statues sculpted by Matyáš Bernhard Braun. Standing in front of the castle as if they were gazing across the countryside, they represent human vice and virtue.

Excursions

MORAVIA

Moravia is known for its folklore, its traditions and the sweetness of its wines (especially in the south).

Brno

- 196 km (120 miles) southeast of Prague

Brno is the unofficial capital of Moravia. It's the country's second-largest city with around 365,000 inhabitants, and welcomes trade fairs and conventions all year long. Among the famous people who lived in Brno are the geneticist Grégor Mendel, the composer Leoš Janáček and the writer Milan Kundera. Archaeological excavation has revealed that Brno has its roots in prehistoric times. It was a trading village that achieved the status of town in 1243. Enclosed within ramparts in the Middle Ages, it developed into a significant settlement in the 14th century. You can visit the castle on Špilberk hill, which first served as the residence of the Moravian princes in the 13th century, and then became a fortress under the Habsburgs. The Gothic Cathedral of Sts Peter and Paul, with its two finely sculpted spires, is visible from afar. Construction began in 1140 and took 30 years to complete. Refurbished in baroque style in the 18th century, the cathedral is daunting in size: the nave measures 64 m (210 ft). The 16th-century pulpit and a14th-century sandstone statue of the Madonna are particularly remarkable.

In the centre of Brno, the marketplace is known for its baroque Parnas Fountain, designed by the architect Johann B. Fischer von Erlach. It depicts Hercules chaining up Cerberus. The Dietrichstein Palace, housing the Museum of Moravia, dominates the square. At No. 4 is the Reduta Theatre where Mozart performed in 1767. You can also visit the former town hall and climb to the top of its tower.

For a more gruesome visit, see the Capuchin Convent (Kapucínský klášter, Kapucínské náměstí 5), which contains mummies of monks and various illustrious personages such as Baron Trench, who battled against the Turks in the 18th century. Until Emperor Joseph II banned the practice in 1784, the dead were set out to dry and mummify in the sun.

Crypt open daily 9 a.m.–noon, 2–4.30 p.m., Sun 11–11.45 a.m., 2–4.30 p.m. Oct–Apr closed Mon.

The superb Renaissance and baroque façades of Telč's market square.

Excursions

Slavkov u Brna (Austerlitz)

20 km (12 miles) east of Brno

The monument dedicated to peace at Slavkov, also known as Austerlitz, was raised to commemorate the battle waged by Napoleon on December 2, 1805, when he defeated an army of 90,000 Russian and Austrian troops. Every year, the battle is re-enacted at the site. In Slavkov, the baroque castle houses an exhibition dedicated to the life of Napoleon.

Strážnice

South of Brno, they treat wine and folklore in the same manner: with lots of enthusiasm. In Strážnice, to the southeast, grannies ride around on bicycles, dressed in traditional garb, their skirts billowing in the wind. A large open-air museum recalls village life in times gone by. At the end of June the biggest folklore festival in the country is held here.

Mikulov

Near the border with Austria, Mikulov (to the south) is a charming wine-growing town with an imposing baroque castle and an old central square. In summer, very colourful folklore festivals are held here, when whole pigs are barbecued in the town hall courtyard.

Telč

One of the country's gems, this town has been designated as a world heritage site by UNESCO, for its castle and its elongated market square, its gabled houses, Renaissance and baroque façades and arcades. The houses bordering the central square all look alike. One large hall called *mazhaus* served for trade or selling beer. Notice, at No. 15, the pretty corbel construction, with projecting upper floors; at No. 37, the sculpture on the gable end; the baroque façade at No. 59; the sgraffito decoration at No. 61. On the square the "lower" fountain, adorned with the statue of St Margaret, was built in 1611. The other, "upper" fountain, dates from 1827. The castle is rather impressive: see the Renaissance halls with their coffered wood ceilings. Carvings in the Hall of Knights (1570) depict the exploits of Hercules.

Olomouc

This town in northern Moravia was founded in the 11th century. Today it has some 110,000 inhabitants. Take time to stroll in its winding alleys, stopping in the central square, Horní náměstí, to admire the town hall, the astronomical clock, the Trinity Column and the two beautiful baroque fountains.

The Hard Facts

Airport
The Ruzyně International Airport, signposted Letiště) is 17 km (11 miles) from the city centre. Information on tel. +420 220 113 314. You can change money there, and hire a car. There are various means of transport to Prague. Either take a yellow taxi with the sign "AAA" on their doors from in front of arrivals– count on a fare of about 500 Kč to the city centre, or take a minibus with the company Cedaz. Otherwise, there is a bus service; buy a ticket at the airport counter (26 Kč). Bus 119 will drop you off at the Dejvická metro station (terminus of the Line A), and bus 100 to Zličin station (Line B). You can use the same ticket on lines A and B to get to the Můstek metro station in the city centre.

City Tours
A tour in a horse-drawn carriage is the most romantic way to explore the Old Town, to the sound of hooves clip-clopping on the cobblestones. The pickup point is in the Old Town Square. Or take a tour in a vintage car; they wait for customers behind the Astronomical Clock).

In summer, you can take a boat trip on the Vtlava river. Don't forget to take some bread to feed the ducks and swans. Departure from Slovansky Ostove (Slav Island), under the Legií Bridge, just behind the National Theatre, or at the Lesser Quarter end of Charles Bridge.

To discover the city on two wheels, why not rent a bike. City Bike hires out mountain bikes and organizes guided tours (three departures a day, at 11 a.m., 3 p.m. and at sunset. www.pragueonline.cz/citybike

Segway tours are available daily Apr–Oct at 11 a.m. and 3 p.m., and Nov-Mar dependng on weather conditions. Departures from beneath the Astronomical Clock; be there 15 minutes before departure time.

Climate
Summers are very hot, and winters bitterly cold, with temperatures sometimes plunging to −20°C (−4°F) in January and February. Snow is not uncommon during these two months. The best time to visit Prague is, of course, spring. Late summer is usually pleasant, and the colours of autumn suit Prague well. The city is less crowded in October and November.

Currency
The Czech monetary unit is the crown (Kč). Banknotes range

from 50 to 5000 Kč, coins from 1 to 50 Kč. The euro won't be introduced for several years.

Exchange offices in the city centre charge a commission of up to 10%, so you will be better off changing money at a bank, where the charges vary from 2–3%. There are several banks and cash machines on Na Příkopě, and others on Celetná Street. The cashpoint at 33 Na Příkopě (MasterCard, American Express, Visa) operates round the clock, as does the one at the American Express office, 56 Wenceslas Square, open daily 9 a.m.–7 p.m.

Many hotels and restaurants accept payment by credit card.

Driving

When driving, give priority to the right. The speed limits are 130 kph on motorways, 90 kph on national roads and 50 kph in built-up areas. Seat-belts are compulsory; the consumption of alcohol is strictly forbidden.

If you drive on the motorway you will need to buy a special sticker to display on the windscreen, available in post offices, certain garages, or at the border crossing. They are available for 7 days, one month or one year.

Petrol stations are common along major routes, but less predictable on secondary roads.

Car theft is fairly widespread in the country. It is best to park in a surveyed parking lot or the hotel garage. The blue parking zones are reserved for residents. The white zones have parking meters. Never leave anything of value in your car.

In Prague, cars are not permitted to drive on lanes signposted Pěší Zóna.

In the city, watch out for the tramways. Their drivers seem to be blissfully unaware of obstacles, either cars or pedestrians.

Distances:
London 1285 km (788 miles)
Paris 1050 km (652 miles)
Brussels 876 km (544 miles)
Zurich 670 km (416 miles)
Munich 360 km (223 miles)
Brno 98 km (123 miles).

Embassies

Canada
Muchova 6, 16000 Praha 6
Tel.: 272 101 800
fax 272 101 890

United Kingdom
Thunovská 14, 118 00 Praha 1
Tel. 257 402 111
fax 257 402 296

USA
Tržiště 15, 11801 Praha 1
Tel. 257 022 000
fax 257 022 809

Emergencies
Medical emergencies: Tel 155

The Hard Facts

Police: Tel. 158
Fire brigade: Tel 150

Na Homolce Hospital
Roentgenova 2, Praha 5
Tel. 257 272 111
Mon–Fri 8 a.m.–4 p.m.

This hospital, 20 minutes from the city centre, has a good reputation. The reception staff speak Engish and the emergency service functions 24 hours a day. An appointment costs the equivalent of $30.

American Medical Center
Janovskeho 48, Praha 7
Tel. 220 807 756

This small private clinic provides reliable medical services by experienced European and American doctors and dentists. You will be charged about $150 for an appointment.

Entry Formalities
Visitors from EU countries need only an identity card. Otherwise you need a passport valid for 90 days beyond the period of intended stay.

Visitors aged 17 or over, travelling from non-EU countries, may import, duty-free, 200 cigarettes; 50 g perfume or 250 ml eau de toilette, 1 litre alcohol over 22° and 2 litres wine, plus 4 litres wine and 16 litres of beer. There is no limit on merchandise bought duty-paid within the EU.

Festivals
The major cultural event of the year is the Prague Spring music festival. Orchestras, ensembles, singing groups and soloists take over the streets and concert halls of the Czech capital.

At Christmas, numerous small outdoor markets set up their stalls around the big Christmas tree in the Old Town Square.

Intercity Travel
Trains are slow, and it is best to travel by bus. You can obtain schedules from tourist information offices.

Many buses leave from the Florenc coach terminal. For information—in approximate English—try calling 1034; the line is often busy. The best bet is to go to the terminal in person.

As a guide, the journey from Prague to Brno takes 2 hours, and from Prague to Telč 3 hours.

The Florenc coach terminal is open Mon–Fri 6 a.m.–6.30 p.m., Saturday 6 a.m.–1 p.m., Sunday 8 a.m.–3 p.m.

The Cedok agency can help with booking tickets and hotels for stopovers, as well as with car hire:
Na Příkopě 18
Tel. 224 197 372
Mon–Fri 9 a.m.–6 p.m.

Lost and Found
Karolíny Světlé 5
Tel. 224 235 085

Newspapers
Newsagents sell most international titles. For local news, read *The Prague Post*, or *Prague in Your Pocket* which contains cinema and theatre programmes, exhibitions, restaurant listings, etc. See also the Prague Post website: www.praguepost.cz

Opening Hours
Banks open Monday to Friday 8 a.m.–6 p.m.; most shops open 9 or 10 a.m. to 6 p.m.

Orientation
Above house doors, the number on the blue plate indicates the address, that on the red plate gives the registration number.

Post
The main post office, open round the clock except for a break between midnight and 2 a.m., is located at Jindřišská 14 (perpendicular to Wenceslas Square). Instructions are given in English at the entrance; press the button corresponding to the service your require, pick up the numbered ticket and wait your turn. Philately at counters 28, 29 and 30.

Other branches open weekdays 8 a.m.–6 p.m.

Public Holidays
Offices and banks are closed on the following days:

January 1	New Year's Day
May 1	Labour Day
May 8	Liberation Day
July 5	Feast of Sts Cyril and Methodius
July 6	Death of Jan Hus
September 28	Anniversary of the Czech State
October 28	Czechoslovak Independence
November 17	Day of Battle for Liberty and Democracy
Dec 24–26	Christmas
Moveable:	Easter Monday

Public Transport
The Prague metro is fast and clean. There are three lines, A (green), B (yellow) and C (red) (see the map on p. 62).

You can purchase tickets in newspaper kiosks, underground stations or automatic machines. There's usually a queue in front of the ticket machines, which are slow and clunky. It's better to go to the newspaper kiosks down the steps in the Můstek and Muzeum Metro stations. A 26Kč ticket is valid for 75 min Mon–Fri 5 a.m.–8 p.m., 90 min from 8 p.m. to 5 a.m. and at weekends, and you can change lines. A 18Kč ticket is valid for 30 min on one line only, or 5 Metro stations (or 20 min in the bus).

Special tourist passes are available: 100 Kč for 24 hours, 330 Kč for three days, 500 Kč for 5 days.

The Hard Facts

Do not forget to stamp your ticket, as inspections are frequent, and you will be fined 950 Kč if you're thought to be dodging the fare (700 Kč if you pay on the spot).

Safety
Keep alert when you are travelling around, as increasing numbers of pickpockets operate in the underground and trams, usually in groups. You're not likely to find a policeman willing to come to your aid. Keep your money and papers well hidden.

If your credit card is stolen, have it blocked immediately, as Prague shopkeepers rarely ask for proof of identity and anyone can use it. In case of theft, go to the police station at the bottom of Wenceslas Square (Jungmannovo náměstí 9, metro Můstek), where English interpreters will be able to help.

Taxis
Prague taxi drivers are notorious for taking tourists for a ride—in more ways than one. The AAA company is considered to be the most professional:
tel. 14 014.

Telephone
Phone booths operate with cards or coins. The code for the Czech Republic is 420. Area code for Prague is 2, and for Brno, 5.

Tipping
In restaurants, it is customary to leave 10% of the bill, even if service has been painfully slow. Pay the tip along with the bill.

Toilets
For the price of a few crowns, you will find clean public toilets, guarded by an attendant, down the steps at the Můstek and Muzeum metro stations, at either end of Charles Bridge and in the castle (near the entrance to St Vitus's Cathedral).

Tourist Information
The staff of the Prague Information Service (PIS) will help you reserve seats for shows, find accommodation or guides:

Old Town Hall
Staroměstské námesti 1
Mon–Fri 9 a.m.–7 p.m.
Daily 9 a.m.–7.30 p.m.

Main Railway Station
Wilsonova 8
Mon–Fri 9 a.m.–7 p.m.
Sat, Sun 9 a.m.–4 p.m.

Tourist Information Centre
Rytířská 31
Daily 9 a.m.–7 p.m.

More tourist information is available on tel. 12 444 or 221 714 444, Mon–Fri 8 a.m.–7 p.m. and you can also look at the website: www.prague-info.cz

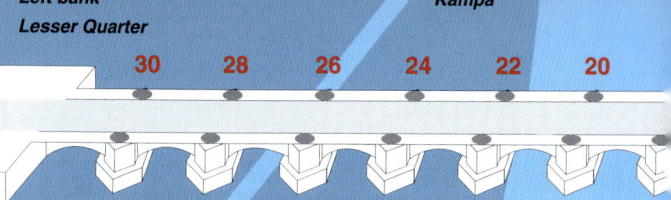

Charles Bridge

Strolling along the bridge is like being in a fantastic open-air museum with its thirty statues looming up on each side. We start our walk from the right bank, Old Town end. You'll need a pair of binoculars to study the intricate details.

1
St Yves, protector of the poor and deprived. At his feet, a mother nursing her infant, an old man and a child begging for mercy. M.B. Braun (1711); copy 1908.

2
St Bernard, the Virgin Mary and two cherubs. M.W. Jäckel (1709); copy.

3
St Barbara (centre), St Margaret (left) and St Elizabeth (right). F.M. Brokoff (1707).

4
St Thomas Aquinas (right), the Virgin Mary and St Dominic (left). The dog symbolizes Dominican inquisitors (Domini canes, God's dogs). M.W. Jäckel (1708); copy 1961.

5
Pieta. E. Max (1859).

6
Crucifixion (1629). The Hebrew inscription in golden letters, Holy, Holy, Holy God, was paid for by a Jew accused of blasphemy (1696).

7
St Joseph. E. Max (1854).

8
St Ann. M.W. Jäckel (1707).

9
St Francis Xavier, supported by two converted Moors, an Indian and a Chinese, with a Moorish king awaiting baptism. The kneeling figure represents the sculptor himself, aged 23. F.M. Brokoff (1711); copy 1913.

10
St Cyril and St Methodius, preaching to three disciples. These Byzantine missionaries began christianizing Bohemia and Moravia in 863. K. Dvořák (1938).

11
St Christopher. E. Max (1857).

12
St John the Baptist with his golden cross. J. Max (1857).

13
St Francis Borgia. F.M. Brokoff (1710); restored 1937.

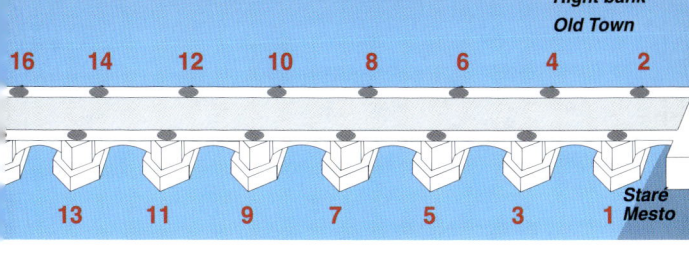

14
St Norbert flanked by St Wenceslas (left) and St Sergius (right), both clad in armour and carrying a sword. J. Max (1853).

15
St Ludmilla, the grandmother of St Wenceslas (c.1720).

16
St John Nepomuk with a halo of five golden stars and a crucifix. Touching the bronze plaque is supposed to bring good luck. Canonized in 1729, John Nepomuk was the queen's confessor, thrown into the Vltava at this very spot when he refused to divulge her secrets to Wenceslas IV (1378–1419). J. Brokoff and M. Rauchmüller (1683).

17
St Francis of Assisi and two angels. E. Max (1855).

18
St Anthony of Padua carrying a golden olive branch. J.O. Mayer (1708).

19
St Vincent Ferrer and St Procopius. F.M. Brokoff (1712). Behind is the statue of the knight Bruncvik, standing guard since 1884.

20
St Jude. J.O. Mayer (1708). In summer, the statue is draped in blossom from the trees on Kampa Island down below.

21
St Nicholas of Tolentino carrying a golden olive branch. F. Kohl (1708); copy 1969.

22
St Augustin with his long beard, mitre and golden staff. J.F. Kohl (1708); copy 1974.

23
St Lutgard, a blind Cistercian nun, kneeling before Christ. M.B. Braun (1710).

24
St Cajetan. F.M. Brokoff (1709).

25
St Adalbert, bishop of Prague. F.M. Brokoff (1709).

26
St Philip Benitius. M.B. Mandl (1714).

27
St John of Matha, St Felix of Valois and St Ivan. A king's son, Ivan lived as a hermit in the suburbs of Prague at the end of the 9th century. Here he is collecting money to buy back the Christians held captive by the Turks and guarded by a dog. F.M. Brokoff (1714).

28
St Vitus. F.M. Brokoff (1714).

29
St Wenceslas. J.K. Böhm (1858).

30
St Saviour (centre), St Cosmas (left) and St Damian (right). J.O. Mayer (1709).

Index

Airport 55
Astronomical Clock 17–18
Austerlitz 54
Beer 44
Beer houses 40
Bertramka – Muzeum W.A. Mozarta 35, 38
Bethlehem Chapel 21
Bohemia 48–51
Brno 53
Cafés 40
Castle 28–32
Castle Square 32
Celetná Street 15–16
Červená Lhota 50
České Budějovice 50
Český Krumlov 50–51
Charles Bridge 22–24, 60–61
Cheb 49
City Tours 55
Climate 55
Clubs 38
Courtyard of the Traders of Tyn 17
Currency 55–56
Czech Music Museum 27
Dancing House 39–40
Driving 56
Dvořák Museum 35
Embassies 56
Emergencies 56–57
Entry Formalities 57
Estates Theatre 17, 37

Festivals 57
Františkovy Lázně 49
Fürstenberg Gardens 26
Golden Lane 31–32
Golem 32
Hergetova Cihelna 26–27
Hluboká nad Vltavou 50
Hotel Evropa 13
House of the Black Madonna, see Celetná Street
Hradčany 27–32
Husova Street 21
Intercity travel 57
Jewish Cemetery 19
Jewish Museum 18–19
– Town Hall 20
Jindřichův Hradec 50
Josefov 18–20
Kafka Museum 26–27
Kampa Museum 25
Karlova Street 21
Karlovy Vary 49
Karlštejn Castle 50–51
Kaunický palác, see Mucha Museum
Klaus Synagogue 19
Klementinum 22
Knights of the Cross Square 22
Kolovrat Gardens 26
Konopiště 51
Kuks Castle 51
Kutná Hora 51
Laterna Magika 37

Ledebourg Gardens 27
Lesser Quarter 25–27
Lesser Quarter Square 25–26
Lesser Square 21
Loreta 32–33
Loretánské Square 32
Maisel Synagogue 19
Malá Strana 25–27
Mariánské Lázně (Marienbad) 49
Mikulov 54
Military Museum 32
Moravia 53–54
Mozart Museum 35, 38
Mucha Museum 14
Municipal House 14–15
Na Příkopě 13
Národní Muzeum 12
National Avenue 13
– Marionette Theatre 37–38
– Museum 12
– Theatre 13, 36
Nerudova Street 27
Nové Město 12–15
Nový Svět Street 33
Obecní dům 14
Observation Tower 34
Old Jewish Cemetery 19
Old-New Synagogue 19–20
Old Royal Palace 30–31
Old Town Square 16
Old Town Hall 17
Olomouc 54
Opening Hours 58

Index

Our Lady Beneath the Chain 24
- of Loreto 33
- of Týn 16–17
- of the Snows 13
- of Victory 25
Palffy Gardens 26
Pařižska (Paris St) 18
Petřín Hill Observation Tower 34
Pinkas Synagogue 19
Post 58
Powder Gate 15
Public holidays 58
- transport 58–59
Puppets 37–38, 47
Rudolfinum 37
Safety 59
St Agnes's Convent 20–21
St George's Basilica 31
- Convent 31
St Giles's Church 21–22
St Nicholas Cathedral (Malá Strana) 26
(Staré Město) 18
St Vitus's Cathedral 29–30
Schwarzenberg Palace 32
Sixt House, see Celetná Street
Slavkov u Brna 54
Slavonic House, see Na Příkopě
Smetana Museum 24
Spanish Synagogue 20
Staré Město 15–18
State Opera 37
Sternberg Palace 32
Strahov Monastery 34
Strážnice 54
Sylva-Taroucca Palace, see Na Příkopě
Tábor 50
Tančící dům 39
Taxis 59
Telč 54
Telephone 59
Tickets 37
Tipping 59
Toilets 59
Tourist information 59
Toy Museum 32
Trade Fair Palace 35
Václavské náměstí 12
Velkopřevorské Square 24–25
Villa Bertramka 35, 38
Vltava 24
Vrtba Gardens 27
Vyšehrad Castle 34–35
Walks 11–12
Wallenstein Palace and Gardens 26
Wenceslas Square 12

GENERAL EDITOR
Barbara Ender-Jones
ENGLISH ADAPTATION
Mark Little
LAYOUT
Luc Malherbe
PHOTO CREDITS
All photos by Renata Holzbachová except:
istockphoto.com/Narvik (inside front cover)
/Rihak p. 1
/Nekrassov p. 11
© Mucha Trust 1997 p. 15
Barbara Ender: p. 45
CARTOGRAPHY
Huber Kartographie
JPM Publications

Copyright © 2009, 1998 by JPM Publications S.A.
12, avenue William-Fraisse, 1006 Lausanne, Switzerland
E-mail: information@jpmguides.com
Web site: www.jpmguides.com/

All rights reserved. No part of this book may be reproduced or transmitted in any form or by any means, electronic or mechanical, including photocopying, recording or by any information storage and retrieval system without permission in writing from the publisher.
Every care has been taken to verify the information in the guide, but the publisher cannot accept responsibility for any errors that may have occurred. If you spot an inaccuracy or a serious omission, please let us know.

Printed in Switzerland
Weber/Bienne — 1163.1.2956
Edition 2009–2010